God's
Word
for
Mothers

God's Word
Word
for
Mothers

BARBOUR
PUBLISHING

Member of the
Evangelical Christian
Publishers Association

Printed in the United States of America.

Introduction

Don't you wish there were a reliable parenting book that covered all the really important aspects of motherhood? A timeless collection of tried and true wisdom that bridged the gap between womb and the woeful teen years? Not to worry! In fact, such a book has been in existence for thousands of years: the Bible.

God's Word for Mothers is a compilation of the very best devotional writing by mothers, for mothers. Drawing on relevant scripture, this collection addresses the emotional whole of motherhood—from stress, exuberance, discipline, finding balance, and everything in between. Whether you're a new mommy or a grandma, God has a lot to offer mothers in His Word. Spend some time today reflecting on your special calling while reveling in the wisdom, laughter, and biblical insight found within these pages.

The Editors

Contents

Family

Reach Out and Touch

She thought, "If I just touch his clothes,
I will be healed."
Mark 5:28

We should never underestimate the power of touch. In our busy lives, as we rush from one appointment to another, skimping on affection with our families and loved ones can become routine. We wave good-bye to our children without stopping for a hug. Husbands head off to work with the barest brush of a kiss.

We do our loved ones a disservice when we skip touching them. Touching communicates our affection but also our affirmation and sympathy. The Bible records Jesus touching many people, comforting and healing them. He also let people touch Him, such as the sinful woman who touched and kissed His feet (Luke 7:38).

In Mark 5, however, the true power of a simple touch is beautifully portrayed. This woman who had suffered for so long believed so strongly in Jesus that she knew the quickest touch of His hem would heal her. She reached out, and her faith made her well.

So hold those you love close, and let them see a bit of Jesus' love in you every day.

Lord, I turn to You when I need comfort. Let me also offer those around me the comfort of a loving touch. Amen.

RAMONA RICHARDS
From *Whispers of Wisdom for Busy Women*

Power over the Plastic

Better is a little with the fear of the LORD,
than great treasure with trouble.
Better is a dinner of herbs where love is,
than a fatted calf with hatred.
PROVERBS 15:16–17 NKJV

Many of us receive more mail from credit card companies than from our relatives! We toss the letters out, but dozens more materialize in our mailboxes with tempting offers.

The pressure mounts as children beg to go to Disney World. Teens sigh for jeans, *the* jeans with perfect designer rips. Meanwhile, the car threatens to give up the ghost. Parents feel so weary, so discouraged. Dinner at a restaurant without cardboard crowns sounds wonderful! All they have to do is hand over the plastic and sign on the dotted line. . . .

God's Word comes to our rescue when we face little temptations that can add up to big trouble. Lovingly He reminds us that unrealistic expectations and overspending can destroy a family. Even macaroni and cheese—again!— with those we love tastes better than costly meals out that strain the budget and rob us of our peace.

Lord Jesus, thank You for Your concern in every area
of our lives. Help us as a family to live within our means
and enjoy the riches of a happy home.

RACHAEL PHILLIPS
From *Whispers of Wisdom for Single Moms*

A Vexation Arises

"Let us not therefore judge one another any more:
but judge this rather, that no man put
a stumblingblock or an occasion to fall
in his brother's way."

ROMANS 14:13 KJV

My mind was ruffled with small cares today,
And I said pettish words, and did not keep
Long-suffering patience well, and now how deep
My trouble for this sin! In vain I weep
For foolish words I never can unsay.

H. S. SUTTON

A vexation arises, and our expressions of impatience hinder others from taking it patiently. Disappointment, ailment, or even weather depresses us; and our look or tone of depression hinders others from maintaining a cheerful and thankful spirit. We say an unkind thing, and another is hindered in learning the holy lessons of charity that thinks no evil. We say a provoking thing, and our sister or brother is hindered in that day's effort to be meek. How sadly, too, we may hinder without word or act! For wrong feeling is more infectious than wrong doing; especially the various phases of ill temper— gloominess, touchiness, discontent, irritability—do we not know how catching these are?

FRANCES RIDLEY HAVERGAL
compiled by Mary W. Tileston

Recipe for Happiness

For wherever there is jealousy and selfish ambition,
there you will find disorder and evil of every kind.
JAMES 3:16 NLT

Give it to me!" Abby shouted.

"No, it's my CD player!" Allyson rebutted.

"You are such a loser!"

"No, *you* are the loser!"

Ahh. . .the sounds of loving sisters. Yes, my girls love each other, but there are days when I have to see that love by faith. Do your children fight? Are there days when you're sure they'll never be friends? Well, take heart. There is hope.

God put your family together, and He knew what He was doing. So even though it may seem like the strife is there to stay, it's not. God is the answer. He can turn your kids into the best of friends in no time at all. Declare that your house is a household of faith. Declare that as for you and your house, you will serve the Lord.

Don't let strife take root in your home, because you don't want to open up your household to every kind of evil as James 3:16 says. Instead, build your house on love. When your kids fight, nip it in the bud immediately. Pray for peace, and watch your family transform. You can have heaven on earth in your home. Start today!

Lord, please help me to keep strife out
of my household. I love You. Amen.

You Look Just Like. . .

For those whom He foreknew
[of whom He was aware and loved beforehand],
He also destined from the beginning
[foreordaining them] to be molded into the image
of His Son [and share inwardly His likeness].
ROMANS 8:29 AMP

Family resemblance. We all have some resemblance to our parents, even if we never saw them due to death or adoption. It could be physical, like the shape of our nose, or it could be in our mannerisms, like the way we walk.

When others tell us how much our children look like us or act like us, we generally respond by saying, "Thank you." For some reason, such comments elicit pride in us.

It's much the same in our Christian experience. Once we've been brought into the family of God, we begin to take on its defining characteristics. Through the Holy Spirit, we are molded into the image of Christ, sharing His mindset and traits. Patience, kindness, compassion, and the desire to please God gradually become part of who we are.

Just as we enjoy the resemblance our own children bear toward us, our heavenly Father wants His children to "look like" Him.

Lord, please have Your way with me.
Cause me to bear the family resemblance.

REBECCA LUSIGNOLO-MCGLONE
From *Whispers of Wisdom for Single Moms*

The House of Babel

*"Let Us go down there and confuse their language so
that they will not understand one another's speech."
So the Lord scattered them from there over the face of
the whole earth, and they stopped building the city.
Therefore its name is called Babylon.*
GENESIS 11:7–9 HCSB

Early in biblical history, the world's people spoke only
one language. They wandered about, came to a plain in
Babylonia, and settled there. Then they decided to build
a tower, a religious symbol, to reach the sky. On top of
this tower there was probably an altar on which human
sacrifices were offered. In punishment, God responded by
confounding their language.

Communication is a powerful tool. But it's often
confounded, even in our homes. There are times when
parents seem to speak a totally different language
than their children! Thankfully, God can cut through
all the miscommunication. He hears and understands
what we're saying, and He speaks to us, too. God says,
"I will instruct you and show you the way to go; . . . I
will give counsel" (Psalm 32:8 HCSB). But that requires
listening as much as talking.

*Lord, unstuff my ears and those of my children!
Help us to listen carefully to Your voice and to each other.*

SUZANNE WOODS FISHER
From *Whispers of Wisdom for Single Moms*

Love Is All You Need

God is love. Whoever lives in love lives in God,
and God in him. In this way,
love is made complete among us.
1 JOHN 4:16–17

Remember that popular '70s song "Love Will Keep Us Together"? Well, there's a lot of truth in that title, especially where our families are concerned.

Life gets complicated, and families fall apart. It happens. It even happens to Christian families. It may have happened in your own family. But I'm here to tell you that love is the answer. When nothing else will, love will keep your family together. No, I'm not talking about that fair-weather kind of love. I'm talking about the God kind of love—an everlasting, unconditional love from heaven.

So even if your teenager has left home or turned his back on God, love will draw him back. Not the sermons you've preached nor the rules you've enforced—only love will turn your situation around. Let God's love live big in you. Let God's love be the superglue in your family, binding you with one another for a lifetime. Live the love and reap the results.

Father, I ask that Your love flow through me to my children. Amen.

Kodak Moments

This is the day the Lord has made;
let us rejoice and be glad in it.
PSALM 118:24

Kodak moments." Aren't they great? I love to look through photographs from past vacations, honor days, field trips, sporting events, family gatherings, holidays, and more! And when I have time, I enjoy scrapbooking—to really showcase our precious pictures. As I was putting together a recent scrapbook, I noticed that almost every picture I'd taken featured smiling, happy folks. Some were posed "cheesy" pictures, but even the candid shots showed intense happiness.

Like the commercial says, those are the moments you cherish. Sometimes you have to hold on to those happy memories to make it through until the next Kodak moment. Life is difficult, and traumatic events can uproot your entire life in an instant. So we need to live each day mindful that these are precious times—treasured times that are gone like the mist in the morning. Enjoy each moment with your children—even the not-so-pleasant ones—and thank God for the Kodak moments.

Lord, I thank You for filling my life with Kodak moments. Amen.

Get What You Give

Finally, be ye all of one mind,
having compassion one of another,
love as brethren, be pitiful, be courteous.
1 PETER 3:8 KJV

Make us of one heart and mind;
Courteous, pitiful, and kind;
Lowly, meek, in thought and word,
Altogether like our Lord.
CHARLES WESLEY

A little thought will show you how vastly your own happiness depends on the way other people bear themselves toward you. The looks and tones at your breakfast table, the conduct of your fellow-workers or employers, the faithful or unreliable men you deal with, what people say to you on the street, the way your cook and housemaid do their work, the letters you get, the friends or foes you meet—these things make up very much of the pleasure or misery of your day. Turn the idea around, and remember that just so much are you adding to the pleasure or the misery of other people's days. And this is the half of the matter which you can control. Whether any particular day shall bring to you more of happiness or of suffering is largely beyond your power to determine. Whether each day of your life shall give happiness or suffering rests with yourself.

GEORGE S. MERRIAM
compiled by Mary W. Tileston

A Labor of Love

*Therefore, my beloved brethren, be firm (steadfast),
immovable. . .knowing and being continually aware
that your labor in the Lord is not futile
[it is never wasted or to no purpose].*
1 CORINTHIANS 15:58 AMP

Cover your mouth!"

"Did you brush your teeth?"

"Don't talk with your mouth full!"

To the casual observer, it may appear that our labor of love—with all of its dos, don'ts, and did yous—has been for naught. After all, how many times should one have to say, "Don't kick your sister!" before Bobby finally gets it? Apparently ninety-eight and counting.

And then there are the deeper issues of life. We teach our kids to treat mean people with kindness, to forgive when they would rather hold a grudge. They're hard lessons to learn, but our labor is not in vain. We have His Word on it.

Raising children to love and honor the Lord is tough work, but the key is never to give in to discouragement. Nothing we do for the Lord is ever wasted. . .even reminding little Bobby to stop kicking his sister!

*Father God, as I raise my children to honor and respect You,
You've promised that my labor is never wasted. What a promise to count on!*

REBECCA LUSIGNOLO-MCGLONE
From *Whispers of Wisdom for Single Moms*

Reflecting God in Our Work

*Whatever you do, work at it with all your heart,
as working for the Lord, not for men.*
COLOSSIANS 3:23

Children are a reflection of their parents. When a mom and dad send their offspring out into the world, they can only hope that the reflection will be a positive one.

As believers, we are God's children. No one is perfect, and for this there is grace. However, we may be the only reflection of our heavenly Father that some will ever see. Our attitudes and actions on the job speak volumes to those around us. Although it may be tempting to do just enough to get by, we put forth our best effort when we remember we represent God to the world. A Christian's character on the job should be a positive reflection of the Lord.

This is true of our work at home as well. No one would disagree that daily chores are often monotonous, but we are called to face them with a cheerful spirit. God will give us the ability to do so when we ask Him.

*Father, help me today to represent You well through my work.
I want to reflect Your love in all I do. Amen.*

EMILY BIGGERS
From *Whispers of Wisdom for Busy Women*

Happily Ever After

*"If you believe, you will receive
whatever you ask for in prayer."*
MATTHEW 21:22

I love to read children's stories that end in ". . .and they all lived happily ever after." Yeah, right! If only it were that easy, eh? In reality, our homes aren't always so happy. A good marriage takes work. A happy home takes work. But both are possible.

We must base our marriages and our families on the Word of God. That's the only way we'll ever have "heaven on earth" in our homes. That's the only way we'll ever experience the "happily ever after." Find scriptures in the Word that apply to your family situations and stand on those.

Begin praying for your husband and your children today. I don't mean just a quick "Bless my husband and my kids" line in your morning prayer. I mean really commit some time to praying for them. You don't have to know exactly what to pray. The Holy Spirit will help you. The point is this—happily ever after *is* possible. Now that's a dream worth having and standing for!

*Lord, thank You for my spouse and my children.
Help me to be the wife and mother You've made me to be.
Please increase the happiness in my home. Amen.*

Household Trials

O LORD, I am oppressed; undertake for me.
ISAIAH 38:14 KJV

Being perplexed, I say,
Lord, make it right!
Night is as day to Thee,
Darkness is light.
I am afraid to touch
Things that involve so much;
My trembling hand may shake,
My skill-less hand may break:
Thine can make no mistake.

ANNA B. WARNER

The many troubles in your household will tend to your edification, if you strive to bear them all in gentleness, patience, and kindness. Keep this ever before you, and remember constantly that God's loving eyes are upon you amid all these little worries and vexations, watching whether you take them as He would desire. Offer up all such occasions to Him, and if sometimes you are put out and give way to impatience, do not be discouraged, but make haste to regain your lost composure.

FRANCIS DE SALES
compiled by Mary W. Tileston

The Least of These

The king will answer,
"Whenever you did it for any of my people,
no matter how unimportant they seemed,
you did it for me."
MATTHEW 25:40 CEV

Some people act as if children are something to be tolerated, not cultivated. They are signed up for this, dropped off for that, and somehow, in the course of all of the activity, they are supposed to learn and grow into adults with a sense of thoughtful purpose. Do we think they'll teach themselves?

Jesus understood the potential of each child. He knew that their little hearts and minds were hungry for knowledge and truth. He knew that their training was an investment in the future of the kingdom of God.

We may never know the full scope of our impact on our own kids, but we are definitely part of God's plan for the development of their young lives. As a mother, you have the potential to bless a child's life forever.

And according to the Lord Himself, whatever you do for a child, you do for Him.

Jesus, use me to shape the lives of my children for Your glory.
Help me to see these kids as a gift from You—never as a hindrance
to my adult pursuits. Please grant me Your wisdom and love.

NICOLE O'DELL
From *Whispers of Wisdom for Single Moms*

Faith

God Cares

Therefore take no thought, saying,
What shall we eat? or, What shall we drink?
or, Wherewithal shall we be clothed?
. . .for your heavenly Father knoweth that
ye have need of all these things.
MATTHEW 6:31–32 KJV

Who is the best cared for in every household? Is it not the little children? And does not the least of all, the helpless baby, receive the largest share? We all know that the baby toils not, neither does it spin; and yet it is fed and clothed and loved and rejoiced in more tenderly than the hardest worker of them all.

This life of faith, then, consists in just this—being a child in the Father's house. And when this is said, enough is said to transform every weary, burdened life into one of blessedness and rest.

Let the ways of childish confidence and freedom from care, which so please you and win your heart in your own little ones, teach you what should be your ways with God; and, leaving yourself in His hands, learn to be literally "careful for nothing"; and you shall find it to be a fact that the peace of God, which passeth all understanding, shall keep (as with a garrison) your heart and mind through Christ Jesus.

From *The Christian's Secret of a Happy Life*
HANNAH WHITALL SMITH

Praise No Matter What

I will proclaim the name of the LORD.
Oh, praise the greatness of our God!
DEUTERONOMY 32:3

Have you ever heard the expression, "Praise and be raised, or complain and remain"? Now that's a phrase that really packs a punch! It means if you complain about your current circumstances, you'll remain there a lot longer than if you'd just praise the Lord in spite of it all.

Sure, that's easy to say, but it's not so easy to do. I don't know about you, but praising God during difficult times is the last thing I want to do. But sulking won't change things any more than complaining will.

By praising God during the dark times, we're telling God that we trust Him—even though we can't see the daylight. Anyone can trust God and praise Him on the mountaintop, but only those who really know God's faithfulness can praise Him in the valley. And it's during those valley times that we truly feel God's tender mercy and experience extreme spiritual growth. So praise God today—even if you don't feel like it. Through your praise, you open the door for God to work in your life.

Lord, I praise You in spite of the difficulties in my life.
Help me to resist complaining and praise You instead. Amen.

In Memory of the Righteous

The memory of the righteous is blessed,
but the name of the wicked will rot.
PROVERBS 10:7 NASB

Not long ago, I attended the funeral of the mother of one of my husband's coworkers. Although I'd never met this man or his mother, knowing that his family had come from the Philippines drew me to the service.

Warmth, love, and appreciation greeted my husband and me from the moment we set foot in the chapel, which overflowed with guests. Somehow, this large family had assembled to provide a magnificent send-off for their precious "Nanay." Amid the battles of World War II, she was widowed at twenty-seven and left with three small children. Yet those difficult days of grief and hardship became her stepping-stones to faith in Christ. Later she remarried and was blessed with five more children.

Her parting admonition to the children who gathered around her deathbed was "Be good and love each other." And then her Lord peacefully escorted her to the mansion He'd prepared.

This woman had lost so much. And yet, blessed with true wisdom, she turned to the Lord for solace and found in Him the foundation on which to build her life. To leave a rich legacy of love, one must be dearly acquainted with the Author of love, our heavenly Father.

From *Daily Wisdom for Women*
CAROL FITZPATRICK

How to Enter In

But thou, when thou prayest, enter into thy closet,
and when thou hast shut thy door, pray to thy Father
which is in secret; and thy Father which seeth
in secret shall reward thee openly.

Matthew 6:6 KJV

$\mathcal{A}$ Christian lady was once expressing to a friend how impossible she found it to say, "Thy will be done," and how afraid she should be to do it. She was the mother of an only little boy who was the heir to a great fortune and the idol of her heart. After she had stated her difficulties fully, her friend said, "Suppose your little Charley should come running to you tomorrow and say, 'Mother, I have made up my mind to let you have your own way with me from this time forward. I am always going to obey you, and I want you to do just whatever you think best with me. I will trust your love.' How would you feel toward him? Would you say, 'Ah, now I shall have a chance to make Charley miserable. I will compel him to do just the things that are the most difficult for him to do, and will give him all sorts of impossible commands.'"

"Oh, no, no, no!" exclaimed the indignant mother. "You know I would not. You know I would hug him to my heart and cover him with kisses, and would hasten to fill his life with all that was sweetest and best."

"And are you more tender and more loving than God?"

From *The Christian's Secret of a Happy Life*
Hannah Whitall Smith

No Worries

"Who of you by worrying can add
a single hour to his life?"
MATTHEW 6:27

If you're an '80s lady, you probably remember that catchy song "Don't Worry, Be Happy." You know, there's a lot of truth in that silly little song.

So many times, as mothers, we think it's our job to worry. After all, if we don't worry about the children, who will? Someone has to worry about their grades, their health, and their futures—right?

Well. . .not exactly. God tells us in His Word that worry is a profitless activity. Worrying about our children may feel like a natural thing to do as a mother, but in reality it's sin. Here's why. If we are constantly worrying about our kids, that means we're not trusting God to take care of them. It's like saying to God, "I know that You created the universe, but I'm not sure You know what's best for my children. So I'll handle these kids, God."

When you put it that way, it sounds ridiculous, doesn't it? We would never say that to God, yet each time we give in to worry, that's the message we're communicating. So do like the song says: "Don't worry, be happy." God's got you covered!

Father, I give all of my worries to You.
I trust You with my children. I love You. Amen.

Knowing God's Precepts

*Teach me Your statutes. Make me understand the way
of Your precepts, so I will meditate on Your wonders.
My soul weeps because of grief; strengthen me
according to Your word. Remove the false way from me,
and graciously grant me Your law.*
PSALM 119:26–29 NASB

Have you ever felt as if you've reached the end of the road
and the only choice ahead of you is a brick wall? When
you reach that point, the only remedy is to look up! God
is waiting for you to come to your senses.

In these verses, we learn the principles that can set things
right. The first, revival, occurs when we truly "seek the Lord
with all our hearts." Martin Luther, an Augustinian monk,
recognized that the precepts he learned from studying the
scriptures didn't mesh with the teachings of the Roman
Catholic Church. Therefore, in 1517, he openly stated his
objections to these teachings by nailing his "Ninety-five
Theses" to the door of the church at Wittenberg. This began
the revival that led to the formation of the Protestant church.

Confession of sin is the beginning of true hope. For
when we acknowledge that we've failed, God can use our
broken and contrite heart, through the Holy Spirit, to
mold us anew.

Understand and walk in the way of the precepts by
meditating on God's Word. If you're not participating in
an in-depth Bible study, consider finding or starting one.

From *Daily Wisdom for Women*
CAROL FITZPATRICK

Against the Current

So likewise, whosoever he be of you that forsaketh not all that he hath, he cannot be my disciple.

LUKE 14:33 KJV

You must remember that our God has all knowledge and all wisdom, and that therefore it is very possible He may guide you into paths wherein He knows great blessings are awaiting you, but which, to the shortsighted human eyes around you, seem sure to result in confusion and loss.

You must recognize the fact that God's thoughts are not as man's thoughts, nor His ways as man's ways; and that He alone, who knows the end of things from the beginning, can judge what the results of any course of action may be. You must, therefore, realize that His very love for you may perhaps lead you to run counter to the loving wishes of even your dearest friends. You must learn that in order to be a disciple and follower of your Lord, you may perhaps be called upon to forsake inwardly all that you have.

Unless the possibility of this is clearly recognized, you will be very likely to get into difficulty, because it often happens that the child of God who enters upon this life of obedience is sooner or later led into paths which meet with the disapproval of those he best loves; and unless he is prepared for this, and can trust the Lord through it all, he will scarcely know what to do.

From *The Christian's Secret of a Happy Life*
HANNAH WHITALL SMITH

How Can We Praise in Faith-Believing?

For we walk by faith, not by sight.
2 CORINTHIANS 5:7 KJV

When the odds seem impossible to overcome, we carefully, painfully seek God's will. But how do we go about actively praising Him in faith-believing?

Faith soars above the mountains of uncertainty and utters a confidence and assurance in our Lord God. He has a precise way of tunneling through, going over or around, and finding the answers. Although we don't know what is around the next bend, we must give Him our unconditional trust.

Putting our faith in action and praising Him for answers to come means plugging up the hill and doing the best we can as we trust Him in the trek. Other times, it is going ahead in faith-believing, knowing without a shadow of doubt what He has for us, even if it's outside our comfort zone! Either way, we must take time to rest our minds and emotions, becoming refreshed in His strengthening Holy Spirit.

The most difficult part for me in putting faith into action and praising Him for answers to come is when I must completely turn all over to God when I hear Him say, "Hands off and let Me."

It is at this point where I learn to actively praise Him for helping, rest in His will and timing, trust Him to fight the battles as I sit back and go along for the ride.

From *When I'm Praising God*
ANITA CORRINE DONIHUE

Trust and Worry

I will put my trust in him.
HEBREWS 2:13 KJV

Remember always that there are two things which are more utterly incompatible even than oil and water, and these two are trust and worry. Can you call it trust, when you have given the saving and keeping of your soul into the hands of the Lord, if day after day you are spending hours of anxious thought and questionings about the matter? When a believer really trusts anything, he ceases to worry about the thing he has trusted. And when he worries, it is proof that he does not trust. Tested by this rule, how little real trust there is in the Church of Christ! No wonder our Lord asked the pathetic question, "When the Son of man cometh, shall he find faith on the earth?" (Luke 18:8 KJV). He will find plenty of work, a great deal of earnestness, and doubtless many consecrated hearts; but shall He find faith, the one thing He values more than all the rest?

Every child of God, in his own case, will know how to answer this question. Should the answer, for any of you, be a sorrowful No, let me entreat you to let this be the last time for such an answer; and if you have ever known anything of the trustworthiness of our Lord, may you henceforth set to your seal that He is true, by the generous recklessness of your trust in Him!

From *The Christian's Secret of a Happy Life*
HANNAH WHITALL SMITH

Take Comfort

For our light affliction, which is but for a moment,
worketh for us a far more exceeding and
eternal weight of glory.
2 CORINTHIANS 4:17 KJV

Do you ever feel your trials are like wearing a crown of thorns? Be faithful. As you trust in God, He will hand you a crown with stars instead. Remember to thank and praise Him.

Do you feel like you are overloaded, your hands filled with heavy cares? Be faithful. As you keep trusting in God, He will take away your heavy cares and place a harp in your grasp, so you may sing glory and honor to God for all He has done. Remember to thank and praise Him.

Hold on and do not despair. There will be a time when you look back and your trials will seem as nothing in light of the many answered prayers, miracles, and evidence of God's glory and grace.

Step by step, day by day, He takes each trial and turns it inside out. Triumphs emerge like a marvelous spiritual metamorphosis. Each of your obedient acts will be transformed to joy unspeakable!

So take heart. Stay faithful. When all is ever so dark, know for sure morning follows the night.

From *When I'm Praising God*
ANITA CORRINE DONIHUE

No Fear

If ye had known me, ye should have known my Father also:
and from henceforth ye know him, and have seen him.

JOHN 14:7 KJV

A friend of mine told me that her childhood was passed in a perfect terror of God. Her idea of Him was that He was a cruel giant with an awful "Eye" which could see everything, no matter how it might be hidden, and that He was always spying upon her, and watching for chances to punish her, and to snatch away all her joys.

With a child's strange reticence, she never told anyone of her terror; but one night Mother, coming into the room unexpectedly, heard the poor little despairing cry, and, with a sudden comprehension of what it meant, sat down beside the bed, and, taking the cold little hand in hers, told her God was not a dreadful tyrant to be afraid of, but was just like Jesus; and that she knew how good and kind Jesus was, and how He loved little children, and took them in His arms and blessed them. My friend said she had always loved the stories about Jesus, and when she heard that God was like Him, it was a perfect revelation to her, and took away her fear of God forever.

The little child had got a sight of God "in the face of Jesus Christ," and it brought rest to her soul.

HANNAH WHITALL SMITH

Dream Big

I can do everything through him
who gives me strength.
PHILIPPIANS 4:13

What do you want to be when you grow up?" I asked my daughter when she was only four.

She thought for a moment and then she answered matter-of-factly, "A movie star."

"Great," I responded. "Then you can pay for Mommy's and Daddy's retirement condo in Florida."

Children know how to dream big. Do you know why? Because no one has told them yet that they can't dream big. I love that about kids. They don't have that inner voice that says, "You can't be a movie star. You're not good enough. You're not pretty enough. You'll never be able to accomplish your dream." No, they believe they can do anything. And you know what? They're right! God's Word says that we can do all things through Christ who gives us strength. All means all, right?

That's why Jesus said we should have childlike faith. We should be able to believe BIG when it comes to the dreams and ambitions that God has placed within us. God wouldn't have placed them there if He weren't going to help us achieve them. So learn from your kids. Get back that childlike faith and start believing.

Lord, help me to believe You like my children believe You.
Help me to dream big like they do. I love You. Amen.

Love

His Wonderful Works

I will praise thee, O LORD, with my whole heart;
I will shew forth all thy marvellous works.

PSALM 9:1 KJV

Audrey loved the little children, and they dearly loved her. She would walk with them through the gardens and fields, showing them all the wonders of nature. She would sit with them for hours and tell them stories. She would read to them from her Bible, then explain what she had read. She would remind the children of all the good things God could do. For the main part of her life, Audrey taught little children the reality of God.

To be truly in love with God is a consuming passion. We can't wait to tell the world of the wonderful truth we know. The Spirit of God enters in, and our lives are never the same again. Praise the Lord with your whole heart, and show forth all His wonderful works.

Each new day brings new wonders to my attention.
Thank You, O Lord, for creating such a beautiful world
with so many miracles to behold. Amen.

From *Wisdom from the Psalms*

Real Love

I trust in God's unfailing love for ever and ever.
PSALM 52:8

We use the word *love* an awful lot. "I *love* your new purse," or "I *love* that dress on you," or "I *love* Hershey's Kisses." I bet if you kept track, you'd find yourself using the word *love* more than a dozen times each day. Because we use it so much, *love* has lost some of its punch, some of its luster, some of its meaning.

But real love—the God kind of love—is so much more than the "love" that has become so clichéd in our culture. The God kind of love is an everlasting love. His love stretches as far as the east is from the west. His love is deeper than the deepest ocean. His love is higher than the highest mountain. His love covers a multitude of sins. His love is unconditional. His love is truly awesome!

Now that's the kind of love I want to walk in. How about you? I want to receive the Father's love, and I want to extend His love to others—especially to my children. As moms, we should have the aroma of love. So if your love aroma is a little funky (like that green cheese in the back of the fridge), ask God to refresh your love today!

*Lord, I pray that Your love—the real thing—
shines in me and through me. Amen.*

Love in Action

Dear children, let us not love with words
or tongue but with actions and in truth.
1 JOHN 3:18

Saying "I love you" to our children is very important. They need to hear those words on a daily basis. But we also need to *show* that we love our children. Have you ever really thought about the common expression "Actions speak louder than words"? There's a lot of truth to that saying.

While it's easy to say "I love you," it's not so easy to show our love all the time. That's why another expression, "Talk is cheap" is used so often. As moms, we need to find ways to back up our "I love yous" every single day. In other words, walk the talk.

Make a conscious effort today to do something special for your children—something out of the ordinary. Leave them little love notes. Make them a special pancake breakfast and serve it by candlelight for added fun. Plan a family night out at one of their favorite places. Just find a unique way to show your kids how much you adore them. Ask God to help you in this area. He will. After all, the Bible says that God is love. He is the expert in showing love.

Heavenly Father, help me to show Your love
to my family on a daily basis. I love You. Amen.

Letting Go

Therefore shall a man leave his father and his mother.
GENESIS 2:24 KJV

My first-grade daughter is still convinced I'm the most beautiful woman in the world. But a few mornings ago, my sixth grader was embarrassed by my appearance.

She was already around the corner, waiting for the school bus, when I noticed her lunch bag sitting on the kitchen table. Without thinking twice, I grabbed it up, and dressed in my sweats, my hair still rumpled from my pillow, I dashed down the sidewalk, my old moccasins slipping and sliding on my feet. "Emily!" I shouted. "You forgot your lunch."

She threw a horrified look at me, and her eyes filled with tears. The other kids waiting for the bus whispered and giggled to each other. I glanced from them to my daughter, and suddenly I realized that I hardly looked my best. And I remembered once more what it felt like to be that age, when each small discrepancy in a person's appearance was fair game for ridicule and laughter. It hurt to know that for the first time in her life, she was ashamed of me.

That day after school, she and I were especially nice to each other. I knew she had forgiven me for embarrassing her. And I forgave her for no longer thinking I was the most beautiful and perfect woman in the world. I guess I was really forgiving her for growing up.

From *Just the Girls*
ELLYN SANNA

Corinthians Conundrum

Love is patient.
1 CORINTHIANS 13:4

Have you ever really meditated on the Love Chapter—1 Corinthians 13? I had to memorize the entire passage when I was a member of our church's high school Bible quizzing team. I wish I lived those verses as well as I can recite them.

You know which one really gets me? "Love is patient." Uh-oh! Patience is one of those virtues that you admire in others but you're sure is not an option for you, right? This is especially true when it comes to our kids. It seems they know exactly which buttons to push. If you're in a hurry, Junior will lose your keys. If you're expecting company, your daughter is sure to spill nail polish on the carpet. If you're on the telephone, every child suddenly needs your undivided attention.

Let's face it—moms get a patience test every day. I've often failed that test. That's why I'm so thankful that God offers "make-up exams." Through His Word and His unconditional love, we don't have to fail those patience tests anymore. The Lord can help us walk in love—even patience—if we'll only ask for His intervention. So ask Him today.

Father, fill me with more of Your love, and help me to have more patience—especially with my family. Amen.

Unconditional Love

*"If you then, being evil, know how to give good gifts to
your children, how much more will your Father who is
in heaven give what is good to those who ask Him!"*
MATTHEW 7:11 NASB

Whether you gave birth or adopted, do you remember the
first time you laid eyes on your child? Their tiny features
instantly enraptured your heart. This parent-child bond
also gave you a glimpse of unconditional love.

What happens to that bond when this little bundle
of joy gets a few years older—and breaks your treasured
vase or gets mud on your new beige carpet? Or when,
as a teenager, your child shatters your heart with hurtful
words and rebellious acts?

Do we tell our children, "You've crossed the line one
too many times. I don't love you anymore"? The idea is
absurd, isn't it?

Yet how often do we fear that our heavenly Father
will react that way with *His* children? If we—imperfect as
we are—have the capacity to show compassion, love, and
mercy to our children, why would our Father in heaven
show us any less?

*Father, please open my eyes to the love and
devotion You have for me. Thank You!*

REBECCA LUSIGNOLO-MCGLONE
From *Whispers of Wisdom for Single Women*

His Favorite

"I have loved you with an everlasting love."
JEREMIAH 31:3

Looking down into the face of my first newborn baby, I couldn't imagine loving anyone more than I loved her at that moment. She was everything I had dreamed of during those nine months of pregnancy. My husband and I did all of the annoying baby talk and silly noises that all new parents do. We were absolutely captivated by her every sound, move, and facial expression. We adored her!

So when I discovered I was pregnant with Baby Number Two on the eve before her first birthday, I wondered, *Can I ever love another child this much?* I was worried. I just couldn't fathom loving another child as much.

Then our second daughter came into this world—bald and beautiful. I looked into her sweet face and fell in love all over again. My husband and I discovered that we could love another baby just as much as our first. We always tell our girls, "You are *both* our favorites!" Do you know that is exactly how God sees us? He doesn't love you or me more than anyone else—we're all His favorites! Meditate on that today and embrace the Father's love.

Father, help me to accept and celebrate Your love for me. Amen.

A Mother's Influence

Direct your children onto the right path,
and when they are older, they will not leave it.
PROVERBS 22:6 NLT

If my mother had been a different woman, I would be a different person. When she read to me each night, I learned about the world of words; today I make my living writing—and I still love coming home from the library with a stack of books to keep me company. When my mother took me outdoors and named the trees and flowers and birds for me, I learned about the world of nature; today, whenever I'm upset or discouraged, I still find peace walking in the woods, and when I recognize ash and beech, trilliums and hepatic, purple finches and indigo buntings, I feel as though I'm saying the names of dear old friends. And when my mother prayed with me each night and before each meal, I learned about an eternal world; today I seek God's presence daily and offer up my life to Him in prayer.

My mother trained me well.

From *Just the Girls*
ELLYN SANNA

Come as You Are

"I have loved you with an everlasting love."
JEREMIAH 31:3

I absolutely love the quirky things about my kids. I love the way they only like purple grape juice because white grape juice just doesn't make sense. I love the way they fall asleep in the car—even if it's only a ten-minute drive to Walmart! I love these little things about my girls because they are my precious children.

Do you know that God feels the same way about you and your quirky little habits? He loves you—everything about you—period! Isn't that good to know?

So many people feel they have to become perfect before God will ever accept them, but that's simply not true. It's a lie that the devil likes to whisper in our ears to keep us from having a relationship with God. The truth is this: God loves us just the way we are! We don't have to be perfect. When we make Jesus the Lord over our lives, He gives us a clean slate. When the Father looks down at us, all He sees is the Jesus inside of us, and Jesus is pure perfection.

*Father, help me to appreciate and celebrate the quirkiness
of my kids the same way that You love and celebrate me. Amen.*

Our First Love

"For I, the LORD your God, am a jealous God."
EXODUS 20:5

Remember your first love? I married my high school sweetheart. I remember the first time we held hands. I remember the first time we kissed. I remember the exact outfit I was wearing when he first said he loved me. I remember it all! Even after twelve years of marriage, I still smile and get all sappy when I hear "our song" on the radio.

God wants us to love Him even more than we love our spouse and children. He tells us that He is a jealous God. He wants us to remember those special times with Him—the moment you gave your heart to Him, the miracles He has performed in your life, the times He came through when no one else could. . . He wants us to sing praise songs to Him as a love offering. He says if we won't praise Him, the rocks will cry out. I don't want any rock doing my praising for me. How about you?

Start today and keep an "I Remember" journal. Record what God does for you each day—even the smallest things. It'll be sort of a daily "love letter" to the Father. If you've grown cold to God, you're sure to fall in love with Him again.

Lord, help me to keep You as my first love. Amen.

The Father Has Bestowed a Great Love

See how great a love the Father has bestowed on us,
that we would be called children of God; and such we are.
For this reason the world does not know us,
because it did not know Him.
Beloved, now we are children of God,
and it has not appeared as yet what we will be.
We know that when He appears, we will be like Him,
because we will see Him just as He is.
And everyone who has this hope fixed on Him
purifies himself, just as He is pure.
1 JOHN 3:1–3 NASB

Have you ever looked into the mirror and thought, *I wish I had a new body?* Well, Christ has one reserved for you in heaven. That body is imperishable, undefiled, and will not fade away (1 Peter 1:3–4).

While we don't know when Jesus is coming again, we do know that our new bodies will coincide with this event. "When Christ, who is our life, is revealed, then you also will be revealed with Him in glory" (Colossians 3:4 NASB).

Yet the gift of our new bodies is only one aspect of the Father's incredible love for His children. His love prompts His children to purify themselves just as He is pure (1 John 3:3). They also abide in Him and practice righteousness (1 John 3:6–7), for they have been born of God (1 John 3:9; John 3:7).

From *Daily Wisdom for Women*
CAROL FITZPATRICK

Harvest Kindness

"If all you do is love the lovable, do you
expect a bonus? Anybody can do that."
MATTHEW 5:46 MSG

Do you realize that we have golden opportunities to show love to others every single day? It's true! When that telemarketer interrupts your dinner and you're tempted to hang up right in that person's ear, don't do it. Show mercy and kindness. Or when you encounter rudeness when checking out at the grocery store, don't return rudeness with more rudeness. No, counter that evil with goodness.

Why? The Bible says we're supposed to do unto others as we would have them do unto us. If we'll discipline ourselves and show kindness when we want to react rudely, God will reward us. This is especially true when it comes to our children. Try it! The next time one of your kids gives you the "whatever" sign and blows you off for no reason, smile sweetly and say, "You are so precious to me. I love you." It won't be easy. Your flesh will want to scream, "Listen, kiddo, you'll not 'whatever' me and get away with it! I am your mother. So don't even go there with me!"

Make kindness a habit. You'll find that if you sow seeds of kindness, you'll reap a mighty harvest of kindness. Now that's the kind of crop I want in my life—how about you?

Lord, help me to show love and kindness
to those who are unlovely and unkind. Amen.

I Love You More Than. . .

"I have loved you with an everlasting love."
JEREMIAH 31:3

I love you more than a million red M&M's."

That's one of our favorite lines from a contemporary movie. It's what the daughter says to her mom in the beginning of *What a Girl Wants*.

My daughters and I have come up with a few of our own "Love you more thans. . ." Here are our top five:

1. I love you more than a bag of Hershey's Kisses.
2. I love you more than a fluffy, fuzzy puppy.
3. I love you more than McDonald's french fries.
4. I love you more than shopping at Limited Too.
5. I love you more than a snow cone with extra flavoring.

This is such a fun game to play on road trips. Also, it's a great way to say "I love you" in a non-mushy, kid-friendly way. As my girls inch toward those preteen years, they tend to become embarrassed by just about everything—especially affection-showing parents.

So find lots of new ways to say you love your children today. Then have each child come up with a new way to express love to our heavenly Father. There's nothing quite like a day of love.

Lord, I love You more than _____. Amen.

The Final Answer

A gentle answer turns away wrath.
PROVERBS 15:1

I recently saw a T-shirt with the printing "Love is my final answer" on it. I thought that was pretty good. Think about it. When you answer with love, you give strife no place to go.

The other day, my daughter wanted to go boating with her friend. Normally we would say yes to this request, but this was a holiday weekend, and according to the news reports, there would be many alcohol-impaired boaters on the lake. We just didn't have peace about it, so we told her, "No, not this time."

She *really* wanted to go, so she began retaliating in a big way. It was ugly. As she huffed and puffed, I decided to try out the "love answer." So I said, "Honey, we love you too much to let something bad happen to you. There will be lots of drunken boaters out there today, and we just aren't willing to take that chance. You are too precious to us." To my surprise, she was okay with that answer. While she was disappointed that she couldn't go to the lake, she understood our reasons and resumed normal behavior. Wow! I didn't even have to raise my voice or threaten to ground her!

Let love be your final answer today. It really works!

*Lord, help me to make love my final answer
in every situation. Amen.*

Prayer

Be Still

Be still, and know that I am God:
I will be exalted among the heathen,
I will be exalted in the earth.
PSALM 46:10 KJV

One morning, the persistent chirp of a mother robin outside our bedroom window awakened me. I glanced at the clock. 4:30 a.m. *How can birds be awake so early?*

I found myself alert, as though a quiet voice were beckoning me to our backyard patio. I slipped on my robe, tiptoed to the kitchen, and quietly prepared a cup of hot tea. I settled into my favorite patio chair—just me, my cup of tea, and best of all, my Lord.

"Be still, and know that I am God." I felt Him whisper on the wind.

I knew I would soon be challenged with endless responsibilities in the next few days. I had already asked for His help. In the solitude of a backyard heavenly chapel, the Lord and I shared secrets, concerns, and direction for an hour and a half. I thought I would be tired. Instead, I felt exhilarated by His Spirit.

Give ear to my words, O LORD, consider my meditation. . . .
My voice shalt thou hear in the morning, O LORD; in the morning
will I direct my prayer unto thee, and will look up.
PSALM 5:1, 3 KJV

FROM *When I'm on My Knees*
ANITA CORRINE DONIHUE

The Doors to Peace

In your patience possess ye your souls.
LUKE 21:19 KJV

How do we find the peace and simplicity we crave in our lives? I think the answer lies in patience and prayer.

We all like to be busy, active, doing; we want to be in control of our lives. But sometimes circumstances force us to accept that we can *do* nothing. All we can do is be patient and pray.

But notice that life has to *force* us to this point. We speak as though patience and prayer were a sort of last resort for people who are too weak or too desperate to do anything else. We turn to prayer only when we are alone and undisturbed, and we practice patience only when we have to. After all, most of us would rather have what we want *now,* not later, and we'd rather be able to get it through our own efforts, rather than wait on God. And so we strive and strive, and our lives become more and more hectic and complicated.

In reality, though, patience and prayer should be our first resort, for they are the tap lines that enable us to find peace even in the midst of life's busyness and noise. They are the doors that lead us into God's peace. And they are the lessons that teach us simplicity.

From *Keep It Simple*
ELLYN SANNA

Depression

The peace of God. . .passeth all understanding.
PHILIPPIANS 4:7 KJV

My nights are sleepless again, dear Lord. Shadows creep around my room. I toss and turn in anguish. When I finally do sleep, I bolt up in bed, frightened that something or someone is after me.

I realize I need Your help more than ever. Life is too tough for me to handle. Lead me to people who can help. Open my mind to ways for me to overcome this terrible depression.

At times I am so distraught I can't even pray. Yet Your Holy Spirit knows my heart. I know You are lifting my needs to my heavenly Father in words that can never be expressed by any human. I take comfort in that.

Let me give my burdens all to You, my Lord. I must let You carry them for me. Most of all, help me be willing not to take them back.

I know You watch over me and will help me through this. I put my trust in You. I won't depend on my own understanding. I purpose to acknowledge You in every way and be alert to Your direction. Let me not worry. Help me do my best to solve each problem as it comes along and pray about everything, large and small. I thank You for your answers, given according to Your will.

From *When I'm on My Knees*
ANITA CORRINE DONIHUE

Handling Rejection

"Man looks at the outward appearance,
but the LORD looks at the heart."
1 SAMUEL 16:7

Can't Buy Me Love" is a catchy little song with a power-packed message. Of course, kids don't always agree with its message. When my husband told our daughters he wouldn't buy them a go-kart, they cried and said, "You just don't love us!"

Maybe you've heard that same retaliation in your home. It's a common kid manipulation, but totally ineffective and way off base. In fact, the reason we wouldn't buy our daughters the go-kart is because it was dangerous for them to have one in our neighborhood. It wasn't that we didn't want to get them one; it's that we wanted to protect them from dangers they didn't understand.

God is like that, too. As our heavenly Father, He has to say no to some of our requests. He sees those hidden dangers that we don't. But when He says no, occasionally I'll come out with that old manipulation that never works—"You didn't answer my prayer, so You must not love me." Of course, that is not true. I know that in my heart, but sometimes I pray out of hurt. I'm so thankful that God looks on the heart, not the hurt. Show your kids that same mercy the next time they say, "You just don't love me."

Lord, help me to show Your mercy to my children. Amen.

God's Voice

Be still, and know that I am God.
PSALM 46:10 KJV

How wonderful it is when God speaks to our hearts. He warns us of entrapments and consoles us in sadness. How satisfying to feel the warmth of His approval when we've done right.

Sometimes we get so busy we unknowingly tune God out, just like flipping the switch on the car radio. He wants us to stay in tune. Each time we listen carefully for His still, small voice throughout the day, we experience joy and peace. Then we are thankful we listened. He helps us avoid a lot of mistakes and heartaches.

When we pray, we are tempted to whisper a quick prayer, jump up, and go about our duties. We assume God's power is with us. How can it be unless we have tuned in?

I've caught myself doing this. It isn't long until my life becomes like one of the old 78 rpm records with the hole not quite in the center. How confusing everything is. I have learned the hard way to pause a little longer after I've said my part in praying, to let God speak to me. The communication goes both ways. When we listen, it completes the glorious circle of our friendship and love.

The next time you pray, remember SAL: Stop, Acknowledge Him, and Listen. Then we can go and serve.

From *When I'm Praising God*
ANITA CORRINE DONIHUE

As Close as a Prayer

How long wilt thou forget me, O LORD? for ever?
how long wilt thou hide thy face from me?
PSALM 13:1 KJV

There is no worse feeling than feeling a distance from God. When we cry out in prayer, we need to feel His presence with us. When that feeling is absent, hopelessness and despair set in. We need to know, however, that the Lord has not really gone far from us, but we have pushed Him from ourselves. The Lord is always as close as a prayer, and we need to open our hearts to Him, and His presence will be felt once again. The Lord never hides His face from us, though often He will wait, stepping back like the loving Father He is, to see whether or not we can struggle through a problem on our own. God wants to see us grow, and He often has to let us struggle a bit in order to allow that growth to occur. Even in those times of trial, however, the Lord is never far away, and He will not allow us to be tried beyond our endurance.

Help me to know that You are with me in every situation
at every moment of the day. I need Your comforting presence
in my life, O Lord. Without it, I cannot go on. Amen.

From *Wisdom from the Psalms*

The Little Things

Do not be anxious about anything,
but in everything, by prayer and petition,
with thanksgiving, present your requests to God.
PHILIPPIANS 4:6

I have a friend who prays for her children's future spouses every day. And her children are only four and six! I hadn't ever considered doing that, but the more I thought about it, the more it made sense to me. So I've begun praying for my girls' future husbands on a regular basis. I pray that they are being raised in Christian homes, learning about the things of God, and growing up to be godly men. Of course, I wouldn't ever tell my daughters I am doing this because they would totally freak out. It's God's and my little secret. But someday when they get ready to walk down the aisle with the men of their dreams, I'll be able to share my secret prayers with them.

My friend who opened my eyes to praying for my children's future spouses has taught me many things about prayer. She prays about absolutely everything. She prays about things that I wouldn't think to bring before God. But she is seeing great results. She has challenged me to pray more—even about little things—and I'm excited to see God's manifestation in my girls' lives. I challenge you to pray more, too. Don't think it's too insignificant to bring before God. He wants to hear it all!

Thank You, Lord, for caring about every detail of my life. Amen.

Praying for Others

Deliver my soul from the sword;
my darling from the power of the dog.
PSALM 22:20 KJV

Perhaps the most pleasing prayer that we offer to God is the prayer that we pray for someone else. A prayer for another person is an unselfish and caring act. It takes the trust we have in God and extends it outward in behalf of other people. It is an example of how we can walk in the footsteps of Jesus. Certainly, God wants us to pray for our personal needs, but we enter into His ministry and love when we send forth our prayers in the names of others.

Hear the concerns of my heart, Almighty God. I care for
so many people, and I want to lift them up to Your care.
Be with them and give them the blessings that You continue
to give to me. Make Yourself real in their lives, Lord. Amen.

From *Wisdom from the Psalms*

True Desires

Delight thyself also in the LORD;
and he shall give thee the desires of thine heart.

PSALM 37:4 KJV

I remember thinking, when I first became a Christian, how wonderful prayer would be. All I would have to do was let God know what I wanted, and He promised that I would have it. I began searching my life for the true desires of my heart, and was surprised to find that they weren't cars, money, or houses, but love, peace of mind, and happiness. The more I prayed, the more I became aware that the true desires of my heart were the desires of Jesus' own heart. They had been there all along, but I had never recognized them before.

Prayer is not a way for us to make ourselves wealthy and prosperous. The Christian's mind should be set on higher things. When we pray to the Lord, always remembering to say, "Thy will be done," we will find the truth of Christ squarely centered in our lives.

There are few people I would rather spend
my time with than You, Lord, though
often I don't spend time with You as I should.
Forgive me when I forget to turn to You.
Make Your desires my desires. Amen.

From *Wisdom from the Psalms*

Take Time

Evening, and morning, and at noon, will I pray,
and cry aloud: and he shall hear my voice.

PSALM 55:17 KJV

Table grace was originally intended to help people turn their attention to God. The meals we share are a gift from God, and He is to be thanked, but we are also to reflect on the many other good things we are given. By praying morning and noon and night, we cover our day with a knowledge of God's presence and abiding love. We should take every opportunity to sing praises to God for all that He has done. Take time to pray. Make time to share your life with God.

Father, I get so busy that I sometimes forget to be as appreciative
as I ought to be. Help me to be thankful and attentive to the many gifts
You have given me. All through the day, I will praise You. Amen.

From *Wisdom from the Psalms*

Bedtime Blessings

But when you pray, go into your room, close the door
and pray to your Father, who is unseen.
MATTHEW 6:6

Do you have a sort of bedtime ritual with your children? Some parents read a storybook to their children every night. Other parents share a Bible story or two. Some even make up their own stories to share. Whatever your bedtime routine might be, I hope that prayer is part of it.

Saying a bedtime prayer with your children is one of the most important things you can do for them. It accomplishes several things, such as teaching your kids to pray by hearing you pray aloud, giving prayer a place of importance in their lives, making prayer a habit for them, drawing the family unit closer, and enriching their spiritual side. To put it in the words of my daughter, "Prayer rocks!"

We spend so much time just doing "stuff" with our kids—running them to soccer practice, helping with homework, playing board games—and all of that is good. But if we don't figure prayer time into the daily equation, we're just spinning our wheels. Prayer time is a precious time. Don't miss out on it even one night. It's a habit worth forming!

Father, help me to teach my children
the importance of prayer time. Amen.

What Is Prayer?

O my God, I cry in the day time, but thou hearest not;
and in the night season, and am not silent.
PSALM 22:2 KJV

Prayer is a tricky thing. It was never meant as a "gimme" list by which we can get things from God. It is not a gripe time to vent frustrations and woes. It is not a time to show off our piety. Rather, it is a time to draw close to God in order to be open to His will and guidance. So often we feel that God is not listening because we don't get what we ask for. We want results immediately, and we decide beforehand what we will accept as an answer and what we will not. Who says we get to make the rules? The Lord hears us, and He is true to answer us, but He always measures His responses according to His divine wisdom. He knows what is best for us, even when it doesn't agree with what we want. It is natural and human to doubt the Lord sometimes. He understands that. Just don't give up. The Lord breaks through our desert spots to comfort us when we cry.

Lift me, Lord, into Your loving arms. Grace me
with the sweet memory of Your care, that I might
never doubt You in times of trial. Amen.

From *Wisdom from the Psalms*

Discipline

Imperfect Behavior, Perfect Love

So let us come boldly to the throne of our
gracious God. There we will receive his mercy,
and we will find grace to help us when we need it most.
HEBREWS 4:16 NLT

We have a system at our house. We keep a "Good Behavior Chart" on the fridge, and that chart keeps track of our daughters' good deeds and completion of assigned chores. Earning As on report cards is worth several check marks. But mouthy, disrespectful attitudes earn several Xs, which cancel out the check marks. This system really works! When the girls wanted to get their ears pierced, we challenged them to earn twenty-five marks. It wasn't long before both of them had met their quota, and we were off to the mall for an ear-piercing celebration.

Aren't you glad that God doesn't have a check mark system? We can never earn our way to heaven. We can't be good enough—no matter how hard we try. It's only by God's grace and mercy that we get in on all of His promises.

As a child, I thought I had to be good all the time in order for God to love me. That's a warped perception of God, isn't it? Let's make sure that our kids know that God loves them—even when they don't behave perfectly. Let's make sure they know that God isn't out to get them—He's out to love them.

Thank You, Father, for loving me even when I behave badly. Amen.

Dare to Be Merciful

Have mercy on me, O God,
according to your unfailing love;
according to your great compassion
blot out my transgressions.
PSALM 51:1

Do your kids ever use the "puppy dog eyes" on you? Aren't those killers? As soon as they bring them out, my heart starts to melt. At that moment, no matter what they've done wrong, I am very forgiving. Of course, my children have learned this trick, so they use it often.

But you know, showing mercy to our children is a good thing. I don't mean that we should let them get away with horrible behavior, but we need to discipline in love and emulate our heavenly Father. Aren't you glad that we serve a merciful God? He is never harsh to us when we repent. He doesn't say, "I'm sorry. You've just made one too many mistakes. I'm not going to forgive you this time." Instead, He lovingly whispers, "That's okay. I love you, My child."

I want to be as tender and forgiving with my children as the Father is with me. If we aren't tender with our kids, they won't run to us when they make mistakes; they'll run away from us. We need to discipline them and teach them the ways of God, but we need to do so with love and mercy.

Father, help me to show mercy to my children
as You show mercy to me. Amen.

The Discipline Dilemma

O LORD. . .your laws are righteous, and in faithfulness
you have afflicted me. . . . Before I was afflicted
I went astray, but now I obey your word.
PSALM 119:75, 67

Let's face it: We want our children to rely on us, to like us, to want to be with us more than anyone else.

But the I-want-my-kids-to-like-me syndrome can cause some parents to recoil from even the thought of much-needed discipline. Sometimes we wrongly assume that discipline gets in the way of showing our children love. But the reality is that a lack of discipline is unkind and unloving.

"Before I was afflicted I went astray," scripture says, "but now I keep Your Word." Affliction, apparently, is one thing that created a change in this psalmist's behavior.

It's okay to "afflict" our children—with a loss of privileges or a few extra chores—to teach them a lesson. Of course, our little darlings may not like us at that moment. But ultimately we are showing more genuine love than any amount of "friendship parenting" ever would.

Heavenly Father, I lean on and rely on You to help me parent my child.
Grant me wisdom to know when and what kind of discipline to use.

REBECCA LUSIGNOLO-McGLONE
From *Whispers of Wisdom for Single Moms*

Rise and Repent

He who heeds discipline shows the way to life.
PROVERBS 10:17

That's it. You're in the time-out chair!" I hollered to my then four-year-old daughter. She had rolled her eyes at me one too many times that afternoon. Slowly, she cowered over to the time-out chair, positioned in the corner of her room. She detested time out. Just hearing the words *time* and *out* in the same sentence made her cringe. But as much as she hated it, she spent a lot of time in that little wooden chair. Her rebellious streak simply took over from time to time.

I find myself in God's time-out chair almost as often as my daughter frequented hers as a preschooler. It seems I also have a rebellious streak. But God's time-out chair isn't a place where He puts you to punish you; rather, you put yourself there when you disobey Him. It's a place where the blessings of God no longer flow. I don't like it there any more than my daughter liked her little wooden chair. But the best thing about God's time-out chair is you can get up at any time. All you have to do is repent and move on. So if you're in the time-out chair today, don't worry. Your chair time is almost up.

Father, help me to follow You all the time. Amen.

God's Guidance

A refusal to correct is a refusal to love;
love your children by disciplining them.
PROVERBS 13:24 MSG

Have you ever spent any time with children who have never been disciplined? You know the kind—the ones who run all over a restaurant, scream when they don't get their way, and show disrespect to everyone. We spent some time with one of these children not long ago. This little girl was unbelievable! She broke toys. She intentionally hurt animals. She talked back to her parents. And she disobeyed every direction. I desperately wanted to discipline her, but it wasn't my place. It was her parents' place. Unfortunately, the parents didn't believe in discipline. They apparently read some book about allowing a child to develop his or her own boundaries.

The only parenting book that's truly needed is God's Word. Proverbs 13:24 tells us that we show love by disciplining our children. In fact, that verse clearly states that it is actually a refusal to love if we don't correct our children. So while Junior may not feel loved at the exact moment he is being punished, he is experiencing love.

Don't be fooled by the world's way of doing things. God's way is always the better choice. He knows a thing or two about parenting. After all, He is a parent. So ask Him for wisdom and guidance when it comes to disciplining your children. He has all the answers.

Lord, teach me to be a better parent. Amen.

Taming the Tongue

My brothers, can a fig tree bear olives,
or a grapevine bear figs?
Neither can a salt spring produce fresh water.
JAMES 3:12

We know from the Word of God that the tongue is hard to tame. Of course, I didn't need the Bible to tell me that fact. I am well aware that my mouth is hard to control. Maybe you have that same challenge. That's why this Scripture really brings conviction to me. If you're praising the Lord in church and hollering at your children on the way home, this scripture probably hits home with you, too.

We need to continually ask the Lord to put a watch on our mouths. We need to ask for His help so that we might be good examples for our children. If they see us praising God one minute and hollering at them the next, they will be confused and disillusioned with the things of God.

James 3:9 says, "With the tongue we praise our Lord and Father, and with it we curse men, who have been made in God's likeness." We must be careful of our words because not only are our children listening, but God is also listening. And we'll be held accountable for our words—all of them.

Lord, please put a watch on my mouth that I might speak
only good things. Help me to be a good example
for my children. I love You. Amen.

The Strength to Say No

*The fear of the LORD is the beginning of knowledge,
but fools despise wisdom and discipline.*
PROVERBS 1:7

Nobody likes to hear the word *no*—especially our children! We have a rule at our house that simply states, "No playtime until your homework is finished." Well. . .that's not always a popular rule. Maybe you have the same rule. If you do, I'll bet you occasionally get the same reaction I do—"Mom! Please! I don't have that much homework. I can finish it later. Let us ride our bikes now."

Yes, I have made exceptions to the rule for special outings and parties, but the rule stands most of the time. We have to think "future minded" for our kids because they live in "the now." I know that if they ride their bikes after school, they'll come in tired and grouchy and have no energy left to do their homework. And if they don't complete their homework, they'll make bad grades. And if they make bad grades, they'll have to be grounded. It's a whole chain reaction of negative circumstances, which is why we came up with the "homework first" rule in the first place.

So don't be afraid to stand your ground. Don't cave in to the whining and begging. Your rules are for your children's own good—even if they don't see it that way.

*Lord, give me the wisdom to make good rules and
the authority to implement them and stick by them. Amen.*

Dispensing Wisdom

The rod of correction imparts wisdom,
but a child left to himself disgraces his mother.
PROVERBS 29:15

No matter where you stand on the spanking issue, this verse holds good meaning. You see, it's not so much about the spanking; it's about the wisdom that we impart when we discipline our children.

There are lots of differing opinions about how to discipline our children. Some experts say we should spank them with our hands. Others say we should spank, but only with a paddle. Still others say we should never spank, only punish by other means. It seems there is a new theory every year. So what is the answer?

God is the only true answer. You must seek His face and ask His direction. He will teach you how to discipline your kids. He loves them even more than you do. He won't lead you astray. Just trust Him. Don't get caught up asking lots of people how you should discipline your kids. If you ask a hundred people, you'll get a hundred different perspectives. They don't know any more than you do. Go to the Source. He will impart wisdom to you so that you can impart wisdom to your children. You see, discipline and wisdom go hand in hand.

Lord, teach me the best way to discipline my children. Amen.

God's Way

"As for God, his way is perfect;
the word of the LORD is flawless.
He is a shield for all who take refuge in him."
2 SAMUEL 22:31

It's my way or the highway!" I heard myself shout at my daughter as she stormed out of the room.

We were having a rather spirited discussion about her disobedience. I let her know that she would follow the rules of the house, or she would spend a lot of time grounded to her room—period! At age ten, she wasn't too keen on the whole "grounded for life" scene. So my declaration of "It's my way or the highway!" seemed quite effective.

While it's a catchy phrase, it's not very correct in God's eyes. It's not my goal to parent my children my way, because my way is rarely the right one. My instincts are often wrong, and I'm way too emotional to make good, solid decisions every time. God's way is *way* more effective. Funny, though, how I sometimes forget that until I've already tried it my way and fallen flat on my face. Ever been there?

So if you're trying to handle everything on your own today—don't! Give it to God. Ask for His divine intervention. His way is best. After all, He is the Way!

Lord, I want to do things Your way—
all the time. I love You. Amen.

In God's Eyes

Before I formed you in the womb I knew
[and] approved of you [as My chosen instrument].
JEREMIAH 1:5 AMP

Okay, I blew it again this week. In my efforts to be a good mother, teaching responsibility and other good morals to my girls, I went overboard. I actually went into the whole "Well, when I was your age. . ." Of course, that's an automatic disconnect for kids. As soon as you utter those words, their eyes glaze over.

Do you ever hear yourself saying something and think, "I've become my mother!" It's so funny, isn't it? One minute, you're hip and cool, and the next parental moment, you're giving your rendition of "When I was a child, we had to walk through the snow, uphill both ways, barefoot to school. . . ."

On those days, when I feel like I'm losing this parental battle, it's nice to know that God has already approved me. Jeremiah 1:5 tells us that He knew us even before we were born and had already approved us. So no matter how badly we mess up, God still loves us and sees us as great parents. He always has His faith eyes in focus. Ask Him to help you get your faith eyes in focus, too. See yourself as God sees you—approved!

Lord, thank You for approving me and calling me to motherhood.
I love You. Amen.

Consequences

"Whoever would love life and see good days must keep his tongue from evil and his lips from deceitful speech."
1 PETER 3:10

When I was a little girl, I lied to my father just once. When he found out, I received a few licks across my backside, but that didn't hurt nearly as much as what my dad said to me. He looked me in the eyes and uttered, "There's nothing I dislike more than a lie. I am disappointed in you."

Whoa! I could handle anything except my dad being disappointed in me. Today, as a mom of two little girls, I've been on the other side of that lying scenario a time or two. And I've discovered that I don't like being lied to any more than my father did.

It's not enough to just tell our children that lying is a sin. We need to take every opportunity to let them know that lying always has consequences. Once when I caught the girls in a lie, I told them that even if they got away with their lie, and I never found out about it, God would always know. That got their attention. You see, they love God, and they didn't want to disappoint Him any more than I wanted to disappoint my earthly father. So strive for honesty in your house. God will be pleased, and that's no lie!

Lord, help me to raise honest, godly children. Amen.

Love More, Yell Less

*I can do everything through him
who gives me strength.*
PHILIPPIANS 4:13

As I climbed into bed, I felt lower than a snake's belly. I knew I had blown it.

My mind replayed all of the times I'd lost my temper with the girls throughout that day. Granted, Abby and Allyson had acted absolutely awful, but I had acted even worse. I wanted to bury my head under the covers and hibernate for at least six months.

Nobody likes to fail, but until we get to heaven, we're going to fail. We're going to have bad days. We're human! I think, as moms, we sometimes forget that fact. We set such high standards for ourselves—so high that they are unattainable by humans. So if you've been feeling lower than a snake's belly lately, take heart! God isn't mad at you. He loves you—temper tantrums and all. Just repent for your wrongdoings and ask Him to help you do better today. You can start fresh right now.

Determine to love more than you yell and laugh more than you nag. If you can do those two things today, you can go to bed tonight feeling really good! You may not be able to do those things in your own strength, but God can help you. Just ask Him.

*Father, I ask for Your forgiveness. Help me to be
quick to love, not quick to yell. Amen.*

A Tale of Tattling

[Love] bears all things.
1 CORINTHIANS 13:7 NKJV

My six-year-old couldn't wait to tattle on her big sister. She was almost bursting with the news, hoping to get her grounded for her misdeed.

"I don't know what your sister did, but before you tattle on her, you'd better be sure it's worth it," I interjected. "Because I ground the one who is exposed, *and* I ground the tattler."

Allyson's eyes didn't look quite as bright as she pondered the temptation to tattle. Slowly, she retreated to her bedroom. Her desire to expose her sister had passed, and I was glad. Tattling is a bad habit that extends way beyond childhood—as adults we call it gossiping. Both are despicable in God's eyes.

Tattling and gossiping are roadblocks in many of our love walks. Exposing each other's shortcomings and failures is the exact opposite of love, because love bears all things. The word *bears* in that sentence means "covers." So the next time your little tattlers run up to you with some juicy information about another sibling, turn 1 Corinthians 13:7 loose on them. Your words may not be effective, but God's Word packs quite a punch! Tattling and gossiping have no place in our homes. Let love root them out!

Lord, help me to raise my children to walk in love. Amen.

Guard Your Joy

For great is the LORD and most worthy of praise.
1 CHRONICLES 16:25

The other day I was at the grocery store, and I noticed a mom struggling with her toddler son. He was doing the whole "I want that toy!" sobbing routine. I smiled to myself, remembering the many times I'd gone through the exact same situation with Abby and Allyson. I felt for her. I wanted to tell her, "It will be all right. Someday, you'll look back on this episode and smile." But I was afraid if I shared those sentimental words of wisdom with her at that moment, she might bop me over the head with the bat her little boy had a death grip on!

We all encounter difficult parenting moments, but if we can keep things in perspective, we'll lead much more joyful lives. When Abby and Allyson used to throw those fits in public, I'd feel humiliated. I'd let the devil steal my joy for several days over one of those crying fits. Looking back, that was wasted time. I should've spent that time enjoying my kids, not beating myself up for their behavior. Don't let Satan steal your joy—no matter how ugly it gets. Just smile and praise the Lord for every parenting moment—good and bad.

Lord, thank You for every parenting moment—even the difficult ones. Help me to keep my joy. Amen.

God's
Promises

Solid Ground

Great peace have they who love your law,
and nothing can make them stumble.
PSALM 119:165

Did you know that God's Word contains approximately seven thousand promises in its pages? It has promises to cover any circumstance or problem that you'll ever encounter. If you're ill and need God's healing touch, the Word says, "By his wounds you have been healed" (1 Peter 2:24). If you're struggling financially, the Bible says, "My God will meet all your needs according to his glorious riches in Christ Jesus" (Philippians 4:19). If your teenagers are rebelling against you and God, the Word says, "But from everlasting to everlasting the LORD's love is with those who fear him, and his righteousness with their children's children" (Psalm 103:17).

No matter what is going on in your life today, God has got you covered. If you can find a promise in His Word, you have something solid to stand on and build your faith upon. Aren't you thankful for that today? God's Word has all of the answers, and we have access to those answers twenty-four hours a day. We live in a country that enjoys religious freedom, so we can even read His promises in public. Praise God for His promises today.

Thank You, Lord, for Your Word. I praise You
for the many promises contained in its pages. Amen.

God's Precious Promises

*His divine power has granted to us everything pertaining
to life and godliness, through the true knowledge
of Him who called us by His own glory and excellence.
For by these He has granted to us His precious and
magnificent promises, so that by them you may become
partakers of the divine nature, having escaped
the corruption that is in the world by lust.*

2 PETER 1:3–4 NASB

From the moment a baby is conceived, it has everything it needs to grow into a complete human being. Our spiritual growth is the same. From the moment we accept Christ, He infuses His Spirit within us, giving us right standing with the Father and making us children of God. "He made Him who knew no sin to be sin on our behalf, so that we might become the righteousness of God in Him" (2 Corinthians 5:21 NASB). As we walk in step with Him, we will eventually reflect these changes in our character.

Peter reminds us that Jesus Christ is the Savior. "Therefore, brethren, be all the more diligent to make certain about His calling and choosing you; for as long as you practice these things, you will never stumble; for in this way the entrance into the eternal kingdom of our Lord and Savior Jesus Christ will be abundantly supplied to you" (2 Peter 1:10–11 NASB).

From *Daily Wisdom for Women*
CAROL FITZPATRICK

In God's Time

I gave you milk, not solid food,
for you were not yet ready for it.
Indeed, you are still not ready.
1 CORINTHIANS 3:2

Do you know that God doesn't dangle carrots just to tease us? No, if God dangles a carrot in front of us, He plans on giving it to us. He would be an unjust God if He placed a dream in our hearts with no intention of helping us achieve that dream. We serve a just and loving heavenly Father. He doesn't like to withhold stuff from us, but sometimes He has to—because we're not ready.

When our kids were babies, they couldn't wait to grow up. They wanted to do all the stuff the big kids were doing, right? But as parents, we had to protect them from the "big kid stuff" because they weren't yet big kids. I remember my daughter wanting to climb the monkey bars at the park so badly. She would stand at the bottom, reach her arms toward the top of the bars, and cry. Her little lip would quiver and my heart would break. But I couldn't let her climb those bars—she wasn't big enough. She didn't know enough.

It's the same way with God. If you haven't yet realized your dream, it's not that God has forgotten you—you just may not be ready yet. If we'll just hang in there, we'll be on the big kid monkey bars before we know it!

Lord, help me to be patient as I wait for my dream to come true.

Drawn to Obey

*For it is God which worketh in you both to will
and to do of his good pleasure.*
PHILIPPIANS 2:13 KJV

God's promise is that He will work in us to will as well as to do of His good pleasure. This means, of course, that He will take possession of our will, and work it for us; and that His suggestions will come to us, not so much commands from the outside as desires springing up within. They will originate in our will; we shall feel as though we desired to do so and so, not as though we must. And this makes it a service of perfect liberty; for it is always easy to do what we desire to do, let the accompanying circumstances be as difficult as they may. Every mother knows that she could secure perfect and easy obedience in her child if she could only get into that child's will and work it for him, making him want himself to do the things she willed he should. And this is what our Father, in the new dispensation, does for His children; He "writes his laws on our hearts and on our minds," so that our affection and our understanding embrace them, and we are drawn to obey instead of being driven to it.

From *The Christian's Secret of a Happy Life*
HANNAH WHITALL SMITH

Work in Progress

For we are God's workmanship,
created in Christ Jesus to do good works,
which God prepared in advance for us to do.
EPHESIANS 2:10

I've always loved this scripture. Did you know that the word *workmanship* indicates an ongoing process? So if we are God's workmanship, we are God's ongoing project. In other words, He isn't finished with us yet! Isn't that good news? I am so glad! I'd hate to think that I was as good as I was going to get.

So if you are feeling less than adequate today, thinking that you are a terrible mother and wife and Christian—cheer up! God is not through with you yet! In fact, He is working on you right now—even as you're reading this devotional. He knew that we'd all make big mistakes, but this scripture says that He created us in Christ Jesus to do good works. He's prepared the road for us. He's been planning our steps long before we arrived here, so don't worry!

We may not be where we want to be today, but as long as we're further along than we were yesterday, we're making progress. We're on the right road. After all, we're God's workmanship, and He only turns out good stuff!

Thank You, God, for working on me, perfecting me from glory to glory.
Amen.

No Shame

But he said to me,
"My grace is sufficient for you,
for my power is made perfect in weakness."
Therefore I will boast all the more gladly
about my weaknesses, so that Christ's
power may rest on me.
2 CORINTHIANS 12:9

Nobody likes to admit weaknesses, but hey, we've all got them. The good news is this—God can work with weakness. In fact, His Word tells us that His power is made perfect in our weakness. Pretty cool, eh? So why is it so difficult to admit we have weaknesses?

I'll be honest, I hate to admit that I have weaknesses—especially with my children. I like to appear perfect and "superhero-like." I want my daughters to think they've got the coolest mom in the world—a mom who loves God, loves them, and can still skateboard with the best of them. But over the past few years, I am pretty sure they've figured out that Mom has got some weaknesses—definitely! The cat is out of the bag, so to speak.

And I'm okay with that. If we let our children see our shortcomings, they'll feel better about their own weaknesses. So quit trying to disguise your weaknesses or make excuses for them. Just admit you've got them and let God's power be made perfect in them.

Father, thank You for working through my weaknesses. Amen.

Christmas Comes on Leaden Feet

A day is like a thousand years to the Lord,
and a thousand years is like a day.
The Lord isn't really being slow about his promise,
as some people think. No, he is being patient for
your sake. He does not want anyone to be destroyed,
but wants everyone to repent.
2 PETER 3:8–9 NLT

To a child, December twenty-fifth takes forever to arrive!

But to a mom, Christmas comes altogether too quickly.

In the first-century church, believers were growing impatient. Jesus had promised to return—but where was He? Like children waiting for Christmas, the early believers couldn't experience Jesus' second coming quickly enough.

God, though, sees time differently than we do. In His love and wisdom, He's giving time to everyone to repent from their sins and truly know Him.

It may seem like Jesus will never return, but the Bible promises He will come and our long wait will one day be forgotten.

It will be a Christmas morning that lasts forever!

Lord of the universe, You are coming back!
May I model patience and expectancy to my family,
never wavering in my belief that You will return!

SUZANNE WOODS FISHER
From *Whispers of Wisdom for Single Moms*

Life-Changing Words

"So shall My word be that goes forth from My mouth;
it shall not return to Me void,
but it shall accomplish what I please."

ISAIAH 55:11 NKJV

I once heard evangelist Kenneth Copeland say, "One word from God can change your life."

It was certainly true for Lazarus when Jesus spoke, "Lazarus, come forth," and he got up and walked out of the tomb, grave clothes and all. It was also true for the little daughter of Jairus when Jesus said, "Little girl, arise," and she stood up after being dead.

The more I thought about it, the more I realized that if one word from God can change your life, then I should be speaking His words into my children at every opportunity. Of course, we can't shove it down their throats like we did those strained peas when they were babies, but we can spoon feed them the Word—a little each day.

And if your children are acting resistant to the Word, don't push. Just let your life show His love, and eventually they'll listen to what you have to say. They'll finally come around. God promises that His Word will not return void, so keep speaking it. That Word will finally take root in their hearts and produce some radical results.

Heavenly Father, help me to find creative ways
to teach Your Word to my children. Amen.

Forgiveness Every Day

Nevertheless my lovingkindness will I not utterly take from him, nor suffer my faithfulness to fail.

PSALM 89:33 KJV

Amy tried everything she could to get the little boy to learn to tie his shoes. She had sat with him for hours. There was nothing she could do to make him understand. Finally, she lost all patience and walked off, mad. His shoe-tying education would have to come from someone else with a lot more patience and endurance!

We may give up on each other, but it is comforting to know that God never gives up on us. His offer of forgiveness is open to us today and every day to come. Even though we reject the offer or do things that are frustrating and displeasing to Him, He never gives up. He asks us daily to follow Him until the day we finally do. Thank goodness His patience is without bounds.

Though I push the patience of others to the limits,
I am glad to know that I have not pushed Yours, Lord.
Continue to forgive me, Lord. I am weak and foolish,
and only Your great love keeps me going. Amen.

From *Wisdom from the Psalms*

He's Watching!

*The eyes of the LORD are on the righteous
and his ears are attentive to their cry.*

PSALM 34:15

Does it seem strange to think that God is watching everything we do? As if He's a traffic cop, hiding behind a billboard, waiting to catch us doing something wrong?

Replace that mental image with the memory of the first time you held your baby in your arms. Or when you watched your child play at a playground. Or act in a school play. Or sing in the church choir. Your eyes scanned the crowd, searching for that familiar little face. You couldn't keep your eyes off your child. *That child belongs to me!* you thought.

God is watching each one of us with the same intense love with which we watch our children. His ability to be near us every moment is no threat—it's a promise. A guarantee! His Word tells us that He is near to everyone who calls out His name. We belong to Him! He can't keep His eyes off us.

*Lord, why is it so hard to believe that You love me?
Your Word reassures me, over and over, yet still, I doubt.
Remind me again, Lord. Convince me!
Draw close! Open my eyes to Your presence.*

SUZANNE WOODS FISHER
From *Whispers of Wisdom for Single Moms*

Sunny Reminder

"Oh, that we might know the LORD!
Let us press on to know him.
He will respond to us as surely
as the arrival of dawn."

HOSEA 6:3 NLT

I'm not much of a morning person. I'm more of a night owl. But it seems that when I travel, most of my flights are very early in the morning. So about three or four times a year, I actually get to see the sun rise. Wow, Texas has the most gorgeous sunrises! Because the land is so flat here in Fort Worth, you get a really spectacular view. God's handiwork is definitely apparent—makes me want to get up early more often!

Even though I rarely see the sun rise, I know that it always does. That's one thing you can depend on—no matter where you happen to be in the world, the sun always rises. That's why I like Hosea 6:3 so much. It says to me, "Hey, as long as the sun rises, the Lord is going to be there for you." Isn't that good news? That means no matter what you're going through right now, God is there for you, ready to respond to your needs.

So every time you see the sun up in the sky, let it be a reminder of God's promise to you. He is there—ready, willing, and able to intervene on your behalf.

Lord, thank You for always being there for me. Amen.

I Won't Worry for the Future

"Who of you by worrying can add a single hour to his life? Since you cannot do this very little thing, why do you worry about the rest?"
LUKE 12:25–26

Sometimes I feel overwhelmed, wondering what the future holds. Then I remember that worry and fear are not from You. I praise You, Lord, for having control of my future.

Why should I be anxious over what tomorrow or the next day brings when I'm Your child and You have my needs and best interests at heart? Thank You for caring for me. Thank You for caring for those I love. I trust that You will be answering my prayers for my loved ones down through generations.

Although Abraham's faith was strong, sometimes he doubted Your promises for his future. Sometimes he created disasters by taking things into his own hands. But You still blessed him and Sarah with a wonderful son.

You have authority over all, so I will not worry for the future. I will trust in You with all my heart and I won't depend on my own understanding. Instead, in all my ways I'll be in tune with You and Your will to guide and direct my paths.

Thank You for the future, Lord. I praise You for going before me and making a way.

From *When I'm Praising God*
ANITA CORRINE DONIHUE

Rest

As Peaceful as a Flower

*Whosoever shall not receive the kingdom of God
as a little child shall in no wise enter therein.*
LUKE 18:17 KJV

We complicate our lives when we borrow trouble from the future. We waste our energy worrying about what might happen tomorrow; we become frantic and pressured looking at the many responsibilities on our to-do list for the next week; we lie awake obsessing over our plans for the upcoming month.

And meanwhile we miss the precious gift of peace that God has given us right here, right now, in this tiny present moment that touches eternity. Be like the wildflowers, Jesus tells us in the Gospels, simply soaking up today's sunshine: "Take therefore no thought for the morrow: for the morrow shall take thought for the things of itself" (Matthew 6:34 KJV).

Children live the same way, delighting in the here and now, untroubled by the future. When we can find that same wholehearted simplicity, we, too, will know the peace of God's kingdom.

From *Keep It Simple*
ELLYN SANNA

In His Arms

I will both lay me down in peace, and sleep:
for thou, LORD, only makest me dwell in safety.
PSALM 4:8 KJV

Sally read until her eyes could no longer stay open. She closed her book, shut off the light, and let her head sink into the comfort of her pillow.

As her eyes closed, Sally's mind began to roam free. *Will seven hours be enough sleep tonight? I didn't get nearly enough done today. . . . I wonder if my car will pass inspection next month. We can't afford a new one. . . .*

Sally shook her head. Frustrated at the turn of her thoughts, she rose up and reached for her Bible. Sally opened up to a favorite verse—Psalm 4:8: "Lay me down in peace, and sleep. . .makest me dwell in safety." She smiled, letting God's Word saturate her mind. Then she fell asleep, cradled in His arms.

Don't let futile worries keep you from catching those forty winks. Fall asleep in God's Word, rest easy, and rise refreshed.

God, with Your Word in my thoughts, I can lie down in peace
and sleep. You will keep me safe, now and forever,
as I rest and then rise in Your power. Amen.

DONNA K. MALTESE
From *Whispers of Wisdom for Busy Women*

Let My Roots Sink Deep

The LORD is my shepherd; I shall not want.
He maketh me to lie down in green pastures:
he leadeth me beside the still waters.
PSALM 23:1–2 KJV

Lord, I sit alone by a quiet stream. My thoughts turn to Psalm 23. The waters gently ripple by. Trees gracefully bow their branches and teasingly rustle their leaves in the pure, fresh breeze. A bird lilts a beckoning call to its mate. A distant falcon pierces the air with its echoing screech.

Peace. Thank You, Lord. But what about when I must return to the hustle and bustle? How can I be prepared?

I look at the trees; their roots sink deep by the stream. In the same way, let my roots sink deep into You. Let me feed on Your Word. As we commune in prayer, let me drink from the living water of Your Spirit. Let me jump in and be bathed by Your cleansing power. I will rely on You rather than things that are shallow and temporary. I can't depend on my own abilities and strength, but I'm confident in Your care and direction.

I will take special notice of the good things when they come. I will fix my mind on what is pure and lovely and upright.

When the heat and winds of life's storms come, I will not fear; I know You are near. I will not worry but keep on producing a life that is a blessing for You and others.

From *When I'm on My Knees*
ANITA CORRINE DONIHUE

A Day of Rest

*Six days thou shalt do thy work, and on the seventh
day thou shalt rest: that thine ox and thine ass
may rest, and the son of thy handmaid,
and the stranger, may be refreshed.*

EXODUS 23:12 KJV

If there is one scriptural principle that women routinely abandon, it is that of the Sabbath. Because Christ has become our rest and because we now worship on the Lord's Day, we often disregard the idea of a Sabbath rest.

Rest was at the heart of the Sabbath. One day out of seven, God's people were not to work or to make others work, so they could all be refreshed.

God Himself started the work-rest pattern before the earth was a week old. God didn't rest because He was tired; He rested because His work of creation was finished.

But a woman's work is never done! How can she rest?

It's not easy. But most things can wait a day while you recharge.

God's design for the week gives rest to the weary. Let's not neglect His provision.

*Father, help me to rest from my labor as You rested
from Yours. Refresh me this day. Amen.*

HELEN W. MIDDLEBROOKE
From *Whispers of Wisdom for Busy Women*

Moments of Peace

"Come to me,
all you who are weary and burdened,
and I will give you rest."
MATTHEW 11:28

Ahhh. . .rest. Who wouldn't love a day of rest? But let's face it. Mothers don't really get a day of rest. If we rested, who would fix breakfast? Who would get the children ready for church? Who would do the laundry so your son can wear his lucky socks for the big game on Monday?

No, there's not a lot of rest in a mother's schedule. But that's not really the kind of rest this verse is talking about. The rest mentioned in this verse is the kind of rest that only Jesus can provide. Resting in Jesus means feeling secure in Him and allowing His peace to fill your soul. That kind of rest is available to all—even mothers.

So in the midst of the hustle and bustle of your life (even if you're elbow deep in dishwater), you can rest in Him. Start by meditating on the Lord's promises and His everlasting love for you. Make a mental list of the things in your life that you are thankful for, and praise God for each one. Allow His love to overwhelm you. . .and rest.

Lord, help me to rest in You—even when I'm overwhelmed with the "to-dos" of each day. I want more of You in my life. I love You. Amen.

Starry Skies

Lift your eyes and look to the heavens:
Who created all these?
He who brings out the starry host one by one,
and calls them each by name.
Because of his great power and mighty strength,
not one of them is missing.

ISAIAH 40:26

Everyone should spend some time stargazing. When we slow the frantic pace of our minds and look to the heavens, we begin to sense the unmatchable power, the sustaining strength, and the intimate love of God. As we gaze with admiration at the stars, we can drink in the very essence of our heavenly Creator.

It was God who hung every star in place. It's God who knows each star by name. Nothing in the farthest reaches of the universe goes unnoticed by God, because He's a God of order and intimacy.

If God cares that deeply about His starry creation, how much greater is His love for us, His cherished daughters?

Father, You are the Creator of all. I thank You that I can take in the awesome vastness of the universe and rest in peace—knowing not only that You are the master Creator, but that You hold me.

KIMM REID-MATCHETT
From *Whispers of Wisdom for Single Moms*

Prioritizing

"If it is the Lord's will,
we will live and do this or that."
JAMES 4:15

I zipped past my father carrying an armload of dirty laundry. A few seconds later, I zipped past with a basket of clean laundry. Ten minutes later, I was wrapping Allyson's birthday presents while talking on the phone. As soon as I put down the receiver, my father sighed.

"You are too busy, honey," he said, sitting in the La-Z-Boy chair, watching *The Price Is Right*.

I realized that I had totally ignored my precious visitor while trying to accomplish the tasks on my to-do list that morning. My seventy-nine-year-old dad had just wanted me to sit down and spend some quality time with him and Bob Barker. So I did. I let the answering machine get the rest of my calls, and I watched TV alongside my dad, making conversation on commercial breaks. Dad has suffered several strokes over the past three years, so every moment we have with him is a precious one.

There are times when those to-do lists serve us well, and there are other times when we need to crumple them up and toss them into the trash. That morning taught me something—don't be too busy with life to enjoy life. It's all about prioritizing, really.

*Lord, help me to prioritize my day in a way
that is pleasing to You. Amen.*

Support Staff

Pile your troubles on God's shoulders—
he'll carry your load, he'll help you out.
PSALM 55:22 MSG

Moms are the unsung heroes, the support staff, the ones everyone depends on. Our purses hold everything from bandages to granola bars to tissues. But there are days when we tire of carrying the weight of the world.

There came a time when Elijah grew tired of caring for Israel. Worn out, he ran for the hills, contemplating early retirement. In fact, he hoped God would give him a break and end it all. "Just kill me," Elijah begged God. He was *that* exhausted.

Was God angry with Elijah for seeking an escape? Did God stand over Elijah, wagging a finger, telling him to pull it together?

Just the opposite! Tenderly, oh so tenderly, God sent angels to care for Elijah. They provided food and rest and encouragement.

Sometimes we're so busy and tired we have nothing left to give. During those times, just let God be in charge for a while.

Dear Lord, teach me to ask for help.
Prod me to take better care of myself.
Thank You for Your gentle response to my low periods.

SUZANNE WOODS FISHER
From *Whispers of Wisdom for Single Moms*

A Good Soak

Oh, how I love your law!
I meditate on it all day long.
PSALM 119:97

Don't you just love to soak in a big bathtub full of bubbles? The beautiful bubbles tickle your toes and the fresh, flowery fragrance fills the room. It's one of my most favorite things to do. If I could, I would soak in the tub so long that my entire body would become "pruney." There's just nothing like a bubble bath—it's pure heaven! It's time well spent, as far as I'm concerned. Soaking in bubbles totally de-stresses me and brings a quiet rest to my soul. And what mom doesn't need more of that in her life?

Do you know what else brings peace and rest? Soaking in God's Word. When you spend time in the Word of God, it transforms you from the inside out. It replaces stress with peace; sickness with healing; anger with compassion; hate with love; worry with faith; and weariness with energy. Soaking in God's Word every day will keep you balanced and ready to tackle whatever comes your way. It's time well spent. You'll become a better person—a better wife and a better mom. And you won't even get "pruney" in the process.

Lord, thank You for Your Word. Help me
to soak it in more and more each day. Amen.

Make Room for Peace

*Let us lay aside every weight, . . .and let us run
with patience the race that is set before us.*
HEBREWS 12:1 KJV

Our society is a busy one. As we dash from responsibility
to responsibility, we seem to pride ourselves on our
busyness, as though it somehow proves our worth. Even
our children are busy, their schedules crammed with
enriching activities.

With such complicated lives, it's no wonder we find
our hearts craving quiet. We long for it so much that
books on peace and simplicity climb the best-seller lists;
we're all hoping some author will have the magic answer
that will show us how to infuse our lives with serenity.

But we're looking at peace as though it were one
more thing to fit into our lives, as though we could write
it on our to-do list. (There it is, right between *Take the dog
to the vet* and *Pick up the clothes from the dry cleaner: Find
a little peace.*) But that's not the way peace works.

The only way we will find peace in the midst of our
hectic lives is if we make room for it. When we stop
the mad rush, when we say no to some of our many
responsibilities and take the time to come quietly into
God's presence, then, in that simple, quiet moment, He
will breathe His peace into our hearts.

From *Keep It Simple*
ELLYN SANNA

A Little Time with God

"I thank You and praise You, O God of my fathers;
You have given me wisdom and might."
DANIEL 2:23 NKJV

Susan headed out of her house in the same way she always did—in a hurry, double-checking her children's backpacks as she went and reminding them of chores and practices scheduled for that afternoon. "Remember, 3:30 is ballet; 4:00 is soccer. I'll pick you up after school, but I have to go back to work, so—"

She stopped as her coat snagged on a bush. As she stooped to untangle the cloth, the stem bent suddenly, and Susan found herself nose-to-petal with a rose. It smelled glorious, and she paused, laughing.

Susan glanced up toward the sky. "Thanks for grabbing me. I guess I should spend a little more time with You."

God blesses us every day in both great and simple ways. Children, friends, work, faith—all these things form a bountiful buffet of gifts, and caring for them isn't always enough. We need to spend a little time with the One who has granted us the blessings.

Father God, You have given us so much to be grateful for.
Show me a way to spend more time with You,
and help me to grow closer and know You better. Amen.

RAMONA RICHARDS
From *Whispers of Wisdom for Busy Women*

Rocking Chair Relief

He will not allow your foot to be moved;
He who keeps you will not slumber.
PSALM 121:3 NKJV

I think the world needs more rocking chairs. We were at Cracker Barrel not long ago and had to wait for a table. So we all went outside and plopped down in our own rocking chairs. I hadn't sat in a rocking chair since my girls were babies.

With each swaying movement, I was taken back to a precious memory of holding my babies in my arms. Now that they are older, they don't sit on my lap very often. They are far "too cool" for that. Sometimes I long for those rocking chair days. Rocking chairs force you to slow down and enjoy the moment. It's almost impossible to be stressed out while rocking. Sitting in a rocking chair is like cozying up to a close, old friend. There's something very comforting and comfortable about spending time in a rocking chair.

You know, even if you don't have a rocking chair at your house, you can spend some quality rocking time in God's rocker. When I pray to the Father, I always picture Him sitting in a big, wooden rocking chair and beckoning me to sit on His lap. If you need to de-stress today, crawl into your heavenly Father's lap and rock awhile.

Lord, I need to spend some quality time just rocking
with You today. Thanks for loving me. Amen.

Seasons

*To every thing there is a season,
and a time to every purpose under the heaven.*
ECCLESIASTES 3:1 KJV

My husband and I broke away from responsibilities and took a drive to our favorite place, the ocean, for a couple of days. After a brief night's sleep, I awakened early.

I quietly slipped into warm clothes and shoes. Bob already knew where I would go. Before long, my strides lengthened and quickened. I approached the pier.

Responsibilities had been crashing in on my life harder than the breakers hitting the huge rocks before me. I watched the waves roll in. They crashed, sprayed, and flowed out over and over in rhythmic patterns.

"Lord, why must I be stretched so thin? I don't think I can handle it all much longer," I whispered.

The sun peeked above the ocean and reflected its rays across the waves.

"Peace, be still," I felt God whisper on the wind. *"Look at the tide change. It's going out now. To everything there is a time and a season. The hard toil won't last forever. In the meantime—rest."*

God reminded me to praise Him while I watched the waves recede. Cold air rushed about me, but warmth filled my being. His presence comforted, assured me.

From *When I'm Praising God*
ANITA CORRINE DONIHUE

Treading Water

With the crowd dispersed, he climbed the mountain
so he could be by himself and pray.
He stayed there alone, late into the night.
MATTHEW 14:23 MSG

Treading water is not a sign of weakness. It's a tactic swimmers employ before their strength begins to fail. When weariness comes on, the swimmer stops pulling herself through the water, instead gently moving her arms and legs ever so slightly to remain above water. No progress is made while treading water, but time is gained for strength to recover.

Moms often feel like they're drowning—losing strength as the waters overtake them. So "treading water" for a time may be the best choice. We won't make any great advancements during that time—but a conscious decision to take no large steps, address no big issues, and simply rest can be exactly what we need to regroup.

Tread water for a few days, even weeks, if necessary. Reconnect with God through prayer and introspection. Let the Holy Spirit renew your soul and body so you can begin the journey once again with a new vigor.

Jesus, please renew and reenergize me as a parent and as a believer.
Through rest and prayer, please strengthen me and return
me to the vigor I once felt.

NICOLE O'DELL
From *Whispers of Wisdom for Single Moms*

Joy

If You Want Joy

Thou wilt shew me the path of life:
in thy presence is fulness of joy;
at thy right hand there are pleasures for evermore.
PSALM 16:11 KJV

"In thy presence is fulness of joy," and fullness of joy is nowhere else. Just as the simple presence of the mother makes the child's joy, so does the simple fact of God's presence with us make our joy. The mother may not make a single promise to the child, nor explain any of her plans or purposes, but she is, and that is enough for the child. The child rejoices in the mother; not in her promises, but in herself. And to the child, there is behind all that changes and can change, the one unchangeable joy of Mother's existence. While the mother lives, the child will be cared for; and the child knows this and rejoices in it. And to the children of God as well, there is behind all that changes and can change, the one unchangeable joy that is God. And while He is, His children will be cared for, and they ought to know it and rejoice in it. For what else can God do, being what He is? Neglect, indifference, forgetfulness, and ignorance are all impossible to Him. He knows everything, He cares about everything, and He loves us! Surely this is enough for a "fulness of joy" beyond the power of words to express; no matter what else may be missed besides.

HANNAH WHITALL SMITH

Serendipity

A happy heart makes the face cheerful.
PROVERBS 15:13

Can you remember the last time you laughed in wild abandon? Better yet, when was the last time you did something fun, outrageous, or out of the ordinary?

Women often become trapped in the cycle of routine, and soon we lose our spontaneity. Children, on the other hand, are innately spontaneous. Giggling, they splash barefoot in rain puddles. Wide-eyed, they watch a kite soar toward the treetops. They make silly faces without inhibition; they see animal shapes in rock formations. In essence, they possess the secret of serendipity.

A happy heart turns life's situations into opportunities for fun. For instance, if a storm snuffs out the electricity, light a candle and play games, tell stories, or just enjoy the quiet.

Jesus said, "I am come that they might have life, and that they might have it more abundantly" (John 10:10 KJV). God wants us to enjoy life, and when we do, it lightens our load and changes our countenance.

So try a bit of whimsy just for fun. And rediscover the secret of serendipity.

Dear Lord, because of You, I have a happy heart.
Lead me to do something fun and spontaneous today! Amen.

TINA KRAUSE
From *Whispers of Wisdom for Busy Women*

The Early Hours

My voice shalt thou hear in the morning,
O LORD; in the morning will I direct my prayer
unto thee, and will look up.

PSALM 5:3 KJV

The sun had just begun to climb into the sky, and the dew shone brightly on the field below. Though not ordinarily a morning person, Ann always loved those special times when she rose in time to see the sunrise. *On mornings like this, who could doubt that there is a God?* Ann's heart filled with a joy beyond words, and nothing could remove that joy during the day. Taking a Bible, she went to a clearing to sit and to read and to pray.

God gives us special times in order that we might find joy and that we might find Him. He has created a glorious world, and He has freely given it to us. The early quiet of the day is a beautiful time to encounter the Lord. Give Him your early hours, and He will give you all the blessings you can hold.

I raise my voice to You in the morning, Lord.
Help me to appreciate Your new day and use it to the fullest.
Open my eyes to the splendor of all Your creation. Amen.

From *Wisdom from the Psalms*

The Promise of Joy

Weeping may endure for a night,
but joy cometh in the morning.
PSALM 30:5 KJV

Have you experienced suffering? Perhaps you are hurting even now. Tough times are a reality for all of us.

The psalmist David was well acquainted with hardship. Although he was known as a man after God's own heart, at times David was pursued by his enemies and forced to run for his life. He also lived with the consequences of committing murder and adultery long after receiving God's forgiveness. But God is faithful, and suffering is temporary. This is a promise we can claim, as David did, when facing difficulty or depression.

As believers, we can find joy in the Lord even as certain trials persist in our lives. All suffering will end one day when we meet Jesus. The Bible assures us that in heaven there will be no tears.

Your loving heavenly Father has not forgotten you. You may feel that relief will never come, but take courage. It will.

God, where there is anguish in my life, may Your joy
enter in. I ask for grace to face my trials, knowing that in time
You will replace weeping with joy. Amen.

EMILY BIGGERS
From *Whispers of Wisdom for Busy Women*

Joy Is Jesus

And even though you do not see [Jesus] now,
you believe in him and are filled with an inexpressible
and glorious joy, for you are receiving the goal
of your faith, the salvation of your souls.
1 PETER 1:8–9

As children we find joy in the smallest things: a rose in bloom, a ladybug at rest, the ripples a pebble makes when dropped in water. Then somewhere between pigtails and pantyhose, our joy wanes and eventually evaporates in the desert of difficulties.

But when we find Jesus, "all things become new" as the Bible promises, and once again, we view the world through a child's eyes.

We learn that God's joy begins with the seed of God's Word planted in our hearts. Suddenly our hearts spill over with joy, knowing that God loves and forgives us and that He is in complete control of our lives. We have joy because we know this world is not our permanent home and a mansion awaits us in glory.

Joy comes as a result of whom we trust, not in what we have. Joy is Jesus.

Dear Jesus, thank You for giving me the joy of my salvation.
Knowing You surpasses anything and everything else
the world offers. Amen.

TINA KRAUSE
From *Whispers of Wisdom for Busy Women*

Choosing Wisely

Our mouths were filled with laughter.
PSALM 126:2

Amanda stared glumly at the rock-hard turkey parked on the kitchen counter. She'd miscalculated defrosting time; it was now Thanksgiving morning, and the entrée of honor was still obstinately ossified.

The twenty-two-pound bird was too large for the microwave, so she tried the blow dryer. Warm air only deflected into her face. Dunking the bird in a warm bathtub merely cooled the water down, and whacking the turkey with a hammer only intensified her budding headache.

We women often plan perfect family events, only to find out how imperfectly things can turn out. Our reactions to these glitches can make or break the event for everyone. Mom's foul mood sucks the joy from the room.

The Bible says that Sarah laughed at the most unexpected, traumatic time of her life—when God announced that she would have a baby at the age of ninety (Genesis 18:12). At this unforeseen turn of events, she could either laugh, cry, or run away screaming.

She chose to laugh.

*Lord, give us an extra dollop of grace and peace
to laugh about unexpected dilemmas that pop up. Amen.*

DEBORA M. COTY
From *Whispers of Wisdom for Busy Women*

Highly Blessed

Every good and perfect gift is from above,
coming down from the Father of the heavenly lights,
who does not change like shifting shadows.
JAMES 1:17

When my daughters were born, I wrote in their baby books "My Gift from Up Above." That's exactly how I felt about each one of my daughters. As I looked down into their faces, I couldn't believe how blessed we were. I bet you felt the same when you had your children. Whether you gave birth to them or adopted them, they were the best gifts you'd ever received, weren't they?

I remember thinking, *They are so perfect, and I didn't do anything to deserve these precious children. God just gave them to me. He loves me that much!*

God is like that. He just loves to give gifts to us—that's what daddies do.

So even on the days when your little darlings are less than perfect and you're thinking, *I thought that Scripture said the Father only sends good and perfect gifts*—rejoice! You are blessed. Send up praise to the Father for your children, your spouse, your home, your extended family, your friends. God loves sending blessings our way—especially when we appreciate the ones He's already sent.

Father, thank You for every gift that You've sent my way.
I am especially thankful for my children. I appreciate You. Amen.

Praise Him in Song

Take a psalm, and bring hither the timbrel,
the pleasant harp with the psaltery.
PSALM 81:2 KJV

Beth was different when she was singing. Somehow the pressures of the world disappeared when the music filled her head and heart. Her whole life felt somehow lighter, brighter, when she lifted her voice in praise through song. Music was the best expression of who she was and what she believed. Music made God real to Beth.

Music is a universal language. Every culture has its music, and it is revered as one of the finest arts. Music brings people together and can move us closer to God. God loves music and the spirit from which music springs. The quality is not nearly as important as the intention of the heart. Sing out to God, and He will bless you richly.

Music touches my heart in a special way, Lord.
Speak to me through the beauty of music.
Touch me day by day. Amen.

From *Wisdom from the Psalms*

The Little Things

*He blesses her with [children], and she is happy.
Shout praises to the LORD!*
PSALM 113:9 CEV

She had been up all night. Her six-month-old baby had been crying for several hours now. She felt she'd reached her limit when something beautiful happened: The baby stopped wailing, and after a few minutes of rocking, both mother and child drifted off to sleep together.

Sometimes it feels as if this thing called "parenting" is the hardest, most thankless job around. But God reminds us in Psalm 113 that children are truly a blessing. They are His gift to us. The salvation of all humanity arrived in the form of a child—God's Son, Jesus Christ—who would grow up to pay the price for all our sins.

In the midst of the struggle, the little things—a smile, a laugh, a present from our children—can remind us how worthwhile this job of motherhood really is and how happy our children make us. Rejoice in these moments each day. Remember the continual blessings of children, the gift of parenthood, and the joy of both.

*Dear heavenly Father, thank You for the gift of children.
Help me to rejoice in each moment of their lives—especially when
parenthood seems like a difficult task. I praise You, Lord!*

CHRISTAN THOMAS
From *Whispers of Wisdom for Single Moms*

Live in the Moment

The fear of the LORD leads to life:
Then one rests content, untouched by trouble.

PROVERBS 19:23

Have you ever heard the expression "Be happy where you are on the way to where you're going"? If you're always looking to the future with longing, you'll miss the good stuff going on right now. You have to find the right balance.

My daughters do this from time to time. When they were younger, they'd get so many presents for Christmas that they couldn't enjoy the ones they'd already opened because they were so focused on opening the next gift. They would hardly look at the roller skates they'd just received before they were on to the next package. It wasn't until all of the presents were unwrapped that they could actually enjoy the blessing load they'd been given.

Have you been guilty of that, too? Are you looking for the next present to unwrap instead of enjoying the blessing load all around you? It's easy to do—especially if you're in the diaper, teething, can't-get-back-into-your-prepregnancy-clothes stage. Some days it's hard to find the "gift" in all of it, but look closely. There are gifts all around. Enjoy this wonderful motherhood journey. Don't miss a minute of it. Every moment should be treasured. You have to enjoy today before you'll ever really appreciate tomorrow.

Lord, help me to enjoy every minute of this journey. Amen.

A Laugh a Day

On your feet now—applaud GOD!
Bring a gift of laughter,
sing yourselves into his presence.
PSALM 100:1–2 MSG

There's an old saying that "laughter is the best medicine." But it's actually more than that.

The Bible tells us that laughter is a *gift*. We should rejoice in the Lord and bring our gift of laughter to Him.

Sometimes, as a mom, you just have to laugh. Maybe you and your young son have just enjoyed a funny movie together. Or perhaps your teenage daughter thought it would be cool to dye her hair purple. In these cases, laughter can be both a song of praise and a catharsis.

It's important to find joy in the events of everyday life, and you should schedule time to pursue a good laugh after a tough week. Call some friends for a girls' night movie party or curl up with a funny book. Maybe you could listen to a Christian comedian for some good, clean humor and worship through laughter.

Whatever the source, make time to laugh—and send those giggles up to God.

Dear God, thank You for giving us the gift of laughter.
Help me to find joy in my daily life—
and to make time to laugh with family and friends.

CHRISTAN THOMAS
From *Whispers of Wisdom for Single Moms*

Reap Joy

> *"Give, and it will be given to you:*
> *good measure, pressed down,*
> *shaken together, and running over."*
> LUKE 6:38 NKJV

Did you know that God wants you to be happy? He desires for you to live life to its fullest. It doesn't matter that you might be elbow deep in diapers and carpools right now—you can still enjoy life!

One of the main ways you can guarantee joy in your life is by living to give. You see, true happiness comes when we give of ourselves to others—our spouses, our children, our extended family, our church, our community, and our friends. As moms, we're sort of trained to be givers. We give up our careers, many times, to become full-time moms. We give up a full night's sleep to feed our babies. We give up sports cars for minivans and SUVs to accommodate our families. In fact, we'd give our lives for our children.

But sometimes our attitudes are less than joyful in all of our giving, right? Well, rejoice today. God promises to multiply back to you everything that you give. When you step out in faith, you open a door for God to move on your behalf. It's the simple principle of sowing and reaping. And as mothers, we are super sowers. So get ready for a super-huge harvest!

Lord, help me to live to give with the right attitude.
I love You. Amen.

Wisdom

His Magnificent Creation

But thou, O LORD, art a shield for me;
my glory, and the lifter up of mine head.

PSALM 3:3 KJV

I was walking along one day, deeply troubled and feeling quite alone. Pressures and problems seemed too much to bear, and I found nothing to make me feel hopeful. My deep thought was broken by a flutter of wings and a flash of color. A butterfly flitted in front of my face, then alighted on my shoulder. The grace and beauty of the small creature broke through my depression and caused me to smile. The great weight I was feeling in my heart lifted, and I began chastising myself for having been so foolish. In a world where such glory exists, why do we continually allow worldly concerns to occupy so much of our attention? Let God be our glory, and indeed, when we find ourselves most down, He will lift our heads up and show us all the wonders of His magnificent creation.

Lord, protect me from those things that turn my attention from You.
Clear the eyes of my heart so they can focus on the splendor
of Your creation. Thank You for the blessings of this day. Amen.

From *Wisdom from the Psalms*

Wise Women

These older women must train the younger women
to love their husbands and their children.

TITUS 2:4 NLT

It was my first night home from the hospital. My baby was sleeping peacefully in my arms. She was so precious. But as I looked down into her little face, I panicked. I thought to myself, *I have no idea how to raise this little girl. I have a hard enough time just taking care of my husband and myself and our dog!* I remember praying for God to send me help. That prayer was answered by way of my mother. She was (and still is) a constant source of encouragement, strength, wisdom, and laughter.

I've learned so much from my mother. Not only has she taught me about being a mom, but she's taught me how to be a better wife. When my father suffered three strokes over a year's time, I watched in amazement as my mother took care of Daddy. She was so strong and in control, yet so tender toward him. I thought, *Now that's the kind of wife I want to be.*

There is much to be learned from our elders, isn't there? That's why I love Titus 2:4 so much. Maybe your mom isn't a person you turn to for advice—and that's okay. God will send other wise women to be part of your life. Ask Him to do that for you today.

Thank You, Lord, for placing wonderfully
wise women in my life. Amen.

Wisdom Comes from God

He came to His hometown and
began teaching them in their synagogue,
so that they were astonished, and said,
"Where did this man get this wisdom
and these miraculous powers?"

MATTHEW 13:54 NASB

The toughest critics you'll ever encounter are family and friends. The reason is simple: They know you best. When vulnerability swings your trapeze with such speed that your grip loosens, they watch as you fall.

Yes, some will continue to stare, waiting for you to stumble once again, but there will be new faces in your crowd of onlookers. They believe you can reach your goals and make a difference in our world.

Jesus encountered these same narrow-minded pessimists. Ridiculing Him, they said, "Isn't He just a carpenter's son?" Yes, but that carpenter was the Master Builder! For Jesus wasn't Joseph's son, but God's Son.

He came from God, full of wisdom. Those who stood with Him during His earthly ministry had true wisdom and understanding from God. They made up His true family of believers. Today, you obtain wisdom through a personal knowledge of Christ and by studying His Word. For only then can God's Spirit fill you with the wisdom you'll need to find and live out your God-given purpose.

From *Daily Wisdom for Women*
CAROL FITZPATRICK

Eat Your Fill

There is a time for everything,
and a season for every activity under heaven. . .
a time to embrace and a time to refrain.
ECCLESIASTES 3:1, 5

Author Carol Kuykendall tells a story of stopping at a
roadside fruit stand after dropping her son off at college.
As she filled a bag with peaches, the cashier commented,
"Better eat your fill of those peaches. When they're gone,
you won't miss them so much."

Carol felt the cashier had given her wisdom that
applied to more than peaches. She went home, cleared
her calendar of all but necessities for the year, and became
more available for her daughter still living at home.

When her daughter left for college, they were closer
than ever, and she wasn't burdened by regret over missed
moments.

Wise old Solomon observed a certain pattern that
God Himself had set into motion: seasons of nature,
seasons of change in our lives. Instead of fighting that
rhythm, we can embrace it, acknowledging that seasons
are part of God's plan for our lives.

Lord, help us to see our lives with a long view.
Give us Your peace as we face our future, knowing You are in control.

SUZANNE WOODS FISHER
From *Whispers of Wisdom for Single Moms*

A Wonderful Life

My heart panteth, my strength faileth me:
as for the light of mine eyes, it also is gone from me.
PSALM 38:10 KJV

Emma was as old as the hills. She had mothered a dozen children, tended a hundred grandchildren, and no one knew how many great- and great-great-grandchildren. She worked every day of the first ninety years of her life; then she decided to rest. In her 103rd year, she lost her sight, and two years later she was confined to a wheelchair. For a while, she was resentful of losing her faculties, but in time she accepted it. After all, hadn't she lived more than a full life? Hadn't God given her more family than any one woman had a right to have? When all was said and done, Emma had had a wonderful life, and a few inconveniences at the end certainly weren't going to get her down.

We have two simple options when afflictions strike. We can moan about our fate and give up, or we can face it boldly and make the best of it. God grants us the power to become more than conquerors, if we will only choose to use it.

Lord, I know there will be times when my strength fails
and my will is drained. At those times, fill my heart
with Your will and power. Make me a fighter, Lord. Amen.

From *Wisdom from the Psalms*

Treasure Every Day

"Is not wisdom found among the aged?
Does not long life bring understanding?"
JOB 12:12

As we strolled through our local grocery store, my three-year-old found a stuffed animal that she just couldn't live without. I told her no, and that was it. She threw herself on the floor and proceeded to have the mother of all tantrums. My other daughter, who was one at the time, let out some sympathy cries, adding to the scene. Once her breathing returned to normal, we headed to the checkout lane.

It was at that exact moment when I saw this sweet elderly man from our church. He looked into the faces of my little girls and whispered to me, "They are so precious. These are the best years of your life. Treasure each moment!"

I smiled politely, but on the inside I was thinking, *Are you kidding me? Did you just see the tantrum I had to deal with back there? Give me a break!* That was more than seven years ago, but his words have stayed with me.

Those were precious years. I can see that now. Sometimes when I was elbow deep in dirty diapers, I couldn't see it. So if you're in the middle of your children's preschool years, take some advice from the wise old man at my church—treasure each moment.

Father, help me to treasure each moment
with my children. Amen.

Be Happy

A heart at peace gives life to the body.
PROVERBS 14:30

Are you at peace with the person God made you to be?

If you don't have peace within yourself, you'll never have peace with other people. God could send you another mom to be the friend you've been praying for, but if you're not at peace with yourself, that relationship won't work. You've got to be happy with who God made you to be before you can experience healthy relationships.

If you're focused on your imperfections and are constantly wishing you were someone else, you're allowing the devil to steal your peace and replace it with wrong thinking. Don't get caught in that trap. That's a miserable way to live. Learn to celebrate the person God made you to be.

The devil will try to convince you that you're a weak worm of the dust. He'll try to get you thinking wrong about yourself. But you need to declare out loud, "I am a child of the Most High King, and He thinks I'm great."

You may not be happy with every aspect of yourself, but you need to be happy about the basic person God created you to be. When you start practicing that mindset, your peace will return. And that's a great way to live!

Lord, I pray that Your peace overtakes me today.
Change my wrong thinking. Amen.

Turn Your Ear to Wisdom

For the LORD gives wisdom; from His mouth come
knowledge and understanding. He stores up sound
wisdom for the upright; He is a shield to those who walk
in integrity, guarding the paths of justice,
and He preserves the way of His godly ones.
PROVERBS 2:6–8 NASB

Every family has at least one relative who cannot get his act together. It's as though these people have to fall in every pothole in the street because it never occurs to them to go down a different road.

Are you smiling yet? Is someone in particular coming clearly into focus? Now hold that thought.

God's Word says wisdom is truly a gift since it comes from the mouth of God. And all God's words have been written down for us. Therefore, those who refuse to accept God's guidance, who refuse to ask for His wisdom—will never see the light of reality.

Know that if you hold fast to the precepts contained in the Bible, you will walk in integrity. Instead of gravitating toward potholes, your feet will be planted on the straight and narrow road.

Lord, I can't change my relatives, but I can change myself.
So if my head is the one peeking out of the pothole,
please pull me out!

From *Daily Wisdom for Women*
CAROL FITZPATRICK

So Little Time

Come, children, listen closely;
I'll give you a lesson in GOD worship.
PSALM 34:11 MSG

If you could only teach your children ten things before you died, what would you share? Would you teach them to stand up for who they are in Christ Jesus? Would you teach them self-defense? Would you teach them good manners? Would you teach them to give to others? Would you teach them to treat others with respect? Would you teach them how to be a friend?

It's a tough call, isn't it? There are so many things we want to impart to our kids. We want to save them from making all of the stupid mistakes that we made. While we can't protect them from every mistake, we can put them on the road to success and happiness.

We can make the most of every opportunity to teach them about the nature of God—God the Healer, God the Provider, God the Savior, God the Deliverer, God the Great I Am! There are chances every day to share little lessons with our children. Ask the Lord to help you identify those opportunities so that you can take advantage of each one.

Lord, help me to share Your love with my children each day.
And, Lord, help me to take advantage of every opportunity
to teach my kids about You. Amen.

Taking Interest

"*Do not judge, or you too will be judged.*"
MATTHEW 7:1

You're not like other moms," commented one of my daughter's friends. "You rock!"

That may be the highest compliment I've ever received in these thirty-plus years. Abby's friend thought it was cool that I knew all of the words to Aaron Carter's latest release, "That's How I Beat Shaq."

Okay, so that's not exactly a spiritual hymn, but the point is, I had taken the time to be interested in my nine-year-old daughter's musical preferences. While scanning her CDs for offensive language (which results in an immediate eject), I discovered that some of her music was kind of fun. I borrowed a few of her CDs and began listening to them when I power-walked. Hey, you've never lived unless you've power-walked to a Jump5 song!

Besides discovering some fun new tunes, I also discovered something else—taking time to know your kids and their likes and dislikes is very cool. It brings you closer to them. It puts you right in the middle of their world and helps you better understand their turf, their dreams, their struggles, and more. I highly recommend it. It's exciting and fun. And you might just find out that you really like that SpongeBob guy after all. (It's okay; I'll never tell.)

Lord, help me to better understand my kids and their preferences. Amen.

Establishing a Vision

Where there is no vision, the people perish.
PROVERBS 29:18 KJV

Cookbooks without pictures aren't much fun. Simple words on a page typically don't move us to culinary pursuits. But if that decadent New York–style cheesecake recipe is actually pictured, we may *run* to the kitchen!

Moms, too, need an image of what we're trying to accomplish. What do we see as the end result of all our efforts? What does success in our family, our parenting, our career, our spiritual life look like? We need a vision. Without it, we'll probably walk aimlessly through piles of laundry, stacks of bills, and grocery store aisles.

With a clear mental image of the future, we can visualize where all the hard work of parenthood is taking us—and see, in our mind's eye, the big picture of what God is creating in us and in the lives of our children.

Ask God to give you a vision of your ultimate destination. It'll make worlds of difference in your day-to-day labors.

Father God, allow me to see the vision You have established for my family—embed it into my heart and mind.

REBECCA LUSIGNOLO-MCGLONE
From *Whispers of Wisdom for Single Moms*

Listening Versus Talking

"My sheep listen to my voice;
I know them, and they follow me."
JOHN 10:27

It has been said that the Lord gave us two ears and one mouth for a reason: We need to listen twice as much as we speak. However, talking seems to come easier for most of us. Our interaction with others becomes the model for our relationship with the Lord. We can become so busy talking to Him during our prayer time that we forget He has important wisdom to impart to us!

Jesus is our Good Shepherd. As His sheep, we have the ability to distinguish His voice. But are we taking the time to listen? It seems much of our prayer time is devoted to reciting our wish list to God. We need to learn to listen more instead of dominating the conversation. God is the One with the answers. He knows all things and possesses the wisdom we yearn for.

Learning to listen takes time. Do not be afraid to sit in silence before the Lord. Read His Word. He will speak softly to your heart. He will impart truth to your hungry soul. He will guide you on the path you should take. Listen.

Dear Lord, help me learn how to listen and distinguish Your voice.
Speak to my heart so that I may follow You. Amen.

JULIE RAYBURN
From *Whispers of Wisdom for Busy Women*

Just Like Mom

Clothe yourselves with. . .patience.
COLOSSIANS 3:12

Have you ever noticed that everybody seems to have an opinion concerning how you should raise your children? Oh yeah—even the woman at the dry cleaners said I should take away my daughters' pacifiers before long because if I didn't, their teeth would rot. That was an interesting tidbit of information I hadn't counted on when dropping off my "dry clean only" laundry.

Many times you'll receive parenting advice from your own mother or your mother-in-law—whether you ask for it or not. They feel it's their duty to impart their nuggets of knowledge. If you're like me, you sometimes tire of endless advice. You've read the parenting books. You are prayerfully parenting your kids. Admit it—there are times when you want to yell, "Back off! They're my kids, and I'm doing the best I can do!"

But before you verbally attack your mom the next time she criticizes the type of detergent you're using on your baby's garments, pray. Ask God to help you receive everyone's input with graciousness and gratitude. You certainly don't have to follow their advice, but grin sweetly as they relay their theory of potty training. Someday, you'll be the one dishing out advice. It's true, you know. We do become our mothers!

*Father, help me to receive advice with grace
and gratitude. Amen.*

Seek Wisdom, Not Self

When a wicked man comes, contempt also comes,
and with dishonor comes scorn.
PROVERBS 18:3 NASB

The delightful movie *Doctor Doolittle* presented a magical animal called the "pushme-pullyou." Such is the woman who has a divided heart! She can never truly go forward in life.

One young woman whom I counseled certainly fit this description. She'd fallen in love with a worthless wretch of a man and become convinced that she somehow possessed the power to change him. Not only could she not change him; she was also unable to raise her children properly. Because this mother was emotionally paralyzed, her children never received godly examples of faith, integrity, and stability.

Women become vulnerable the instant truth is replaced with desire.

So how can we teach our daughters to be wise? By acquiring knowledge ourselves. As we study and store God's Word in times of peace, our first thoughts during periods of stress or crisis will be Scripture. People falter because they fail to plan. If we just do what God expects of us, despite the magnetic pull of sin, we gain strength of character. Negotiating with evil nets us a zero every time.

Lord, sometimes I want so badly to be loved that I trust the wrong
people. Please guide me to those who are trustworthy.

From *Daily Wisdom for Women*
CAROL FITZPATRICK

Finding Balance

The Virtuous Woman

An excellent wife, who can find? For her worth is far above jewels. The heart of her husband trusts in her, and he will have no lack of gain. She does him good and not evil all the days of her life.

PROVERBS 31:10–12 NASB

When my husband was discharged from active duty with the army, we were thrust into an uncertain economy with a glut of civil engineers out of work. Consequently, my husband had to choose another major.

Dreams of evenings at home together spent with our growing family never materialized as my husband was either at his night-school classes or in the library. The burden fell on my shoulders to keep our children occupied each night. At times, my days with the kids seemed endless, especially since none of them was yet in school.

After the little ones were finally tucked into bed, there were still a couple of hours before my bedraggled husband would reappear. I filled them with my own crafts, letter writing, reading, and Bible study.

The virtuous woman in the Scriptures did good to her husband and not evil. All her activities were geared toward building up her home. This is the example I followed. Years later, when my husband finally graduated with a degree in a new field, his family remained intact.

From *Daily Wisdom for Women*
CAROL FITZPATRICK

Ditch the List

*"But seek first his kingdom and his righteousness,
and all these things will be given to you as well."*
MATTHEW 6:33

Are you a planner? Are you a list maker? You know, my list making became so addictive that I found myself making lists during our pastor's sermon on Sunday mornings. Of course, it looked like I was taking notes, but I wasn't—I was planning out my week.

The pastor was preaching about spending more quality time with God, and I was scheduling a fifteen-minute devotional time for Him somewhere on Thursday. Pretty sad, huh?

Well, I'm happy to say that there is life after lists. I am a recovering to-do list maker. It was a gradual process, but now I can actually sit through a sermon and truly focus on what the pastor is saying.

I've found such freedom in trusting God with my daily activities. Sure, I still have reminder sticky notes scattered around my house, but now I'm not ruled by a list. I've learned there is sweet rest and freedom in trusting God with my day.

So before your feet hit the floor each morning, simply pray, "God I give this day to You." Let Him make your list. Trust me, His list is easier to accomplish and much more fulfilling.

*Lord, I commit this week to You. Help me to plan
wisely and follow Your leading. Amen.*

Finding God in Everyday Life

He shall. . .gently lead those that are with young.
ISAIAH 40:11 KJV

I have made prayer too much of a luxury and have often inwardly chafed and fretted when the care of my children, at times, made it utterly impossible to leave them for private devotion—when they have been sick, for instance, or other like emergencies. I reasoned this way: "Here is a special demand on my patience, and I am naturally impatient. I must have time to go away and entreat the Lord to equip me for this conflict." But I see now that the simple act of cheerful acceptance of the duty imposed and the solace and support withdrawn would have united me more fully to Christ than the highest enjoyment of His presence in prayer could.

From *Stepping Heavenward*
ELIZABETH PRENTISS

Feeling the Squeeze

The eye can never say to the hand, "I don't need you."
The head can't say to the feet, "I don't need you."
1 CORINTHIANS 12:21 NLT

We've all heard the term "the sandwich generation," referring to midlifers coping with teenagers on one end and aging parents on the other. Somehow, calling it a sandwich sounds too easy. The in-between filling seems to fit comfortably, like ham and Swiss on rye. A more appropriate term would be "the squeeze generation." Picture peanut butter and jelly oozing out of squished white bread.

It is a challenging season of life, and we can't do it alone. And perhaps that is a great blessing to realize. God never meant for us to do it alone! He designed us to live in communities—family, friends, and church—that help meet one another's needs. "The body is a unit," Paul told the believers at Corinth, "though it is made up of many parts; and though all its parts are many, they form one body. So it is with Christ" (1 Corinthians 12:12).

There's nothing wrong with asking for help when you need it.

Lord, You promise never to leave us nor forsake us.
Thank You for providing helpers to come alongside of me. Amen.

SUZANNE WOODS FISHER
From *Whispers of Wisdom for Busy Women*

Our Assigned Work

I will surely do thee good.
GENESIS 32:12 KJV

Thou know'st not what is good for thee,
But God doth know—
Let Him thy strong reliance be,
And rest thee so.
C. F. GELLERT

Let us be very careful of thinking, on the one hand, that we have no work assigned us to do or, on the other hand, that what we have assigned to us is not the right thing for us. If ever we can say in our hearts to God, in reference to any daily duty, "This is not my place; I would choose something dearer; I am capable of something higher," we are guilty not only of rebellion, but of blasphemy. It is equivalent to saying, not only, "My heart revolts against Thy commands," but "Thy commands are unwise; Thine Almighty guidance is unskillful; Thine omniscient eye has mistaken the capacities of Thy creature; Thine infinite love is indifferent to the welfare of Thy child."

ELIZABETH CHARLES
compiled by MARY W. TILESTON

Be Carefree

Cast all your anxiety on him
because he cares for you.
1 PETER 5:7

Ever have one of those days? The alarm clock didn't go off. The kids were late for school. The dog threw up on the carpet. You spilled coffee down the front of your new white blouse. Ahhh! It's one of those "Calgon, take me away!" days, right?

But it doesn't have to be. No matter how many challenges you face today, you can smile in the face of aggravation. How? By casting your cares upon the Lord. That's what the Lord tells us to do in His Word, yet many of us feel compelled to take all of the cares upon ourselves. After all, we're mothers. We're fixers. We're the doers of the bunch. We wear five or six fedoras at a time—we can handle anything that comes our way, right?

Wrong! But God can. When the day starts to go south, cast your cares on Him. He wants you to! As mothers, we can handle a lot, but it's true what they say—Father really does know best. So give it to God. C'mon, you know you want to. . . .

Lord, help me to turn to You when my troubles
seem too big to face alone and even when they don't.
Help me to trust You with all of my cares.
I love You, Lord. Amen.

Interruptions

The LORD thy God shall bless thee in all thy works,
and in all that thou puttest thine hand unto.
DEUTERONOMY 15:10 KJV

My place of lowly service, too,
Beneath Thy sheltering wings I see;
For all the work I have to do
Is done through sheltering rest in Thee.
A. L. WARING

I think I find most help in trying to look on all interruptions and hindrances to work that one has planned out for oneself as discipline, trials sent by God to help one against getting selfish over one's work. Then one can feel that perhaps one's true work—one's work for God—consists in doing some trifling haphazard thing that has been thrown into one's day. It is not a waste of time, as one is tempted to think. It is the most important part of the work of the day—the part one can best offer to God. After such a hindrance, do not rush after the planned work; trust that the time to finish it will be given sometime, and keep a quiet heart about it.

ANNIE KEARY
compiled by MARY W. TILESTON

Play More, Plan Less

There is a time for everything,
and a season for every activity under heaven.
ECCLESIASTES 3:1

If they gave an award for "World's Coolest Mom," my friend would win. She's nice and fun, and she throws the most elaborate birthday parties for her little girl. From games to treats to goodie bags—her parties rock!

Just before her daughter's seventh birthday, my friend was at it again. But in the midst of party-planning, her daughter kept asking, "Mama, will you play with me?"

After saying no several times, my frustrated friend answered, "I can't play right now. I'm busy planning *your* birthday party. Now, isn't that more important?"

Her little girl looked up at her and thoughtfully said, "No. I'd rather cancel the party and just have you play with me. That's the best present."

Even as my friend shared the story with me, tears came to her eyes. Her daughter didn't care about an elaborate birthday bash. She simply wanted her mom's attention.

Many times in our quest to be the perfect mom, we lose sight of the big picture—our children need our love and attention more than anything.

Lord, help me to make time for the most
important people in my life, and help me
to keep things in perspective. Amen.

See It and Believe It

So do not throw away your confidence;
it will be richly rewarded.
HEBREWS 10:35

Are you focusing on the future, or are you having trouble seeing past the endless piles of dirty laundry that are in front of you right now? When today has so many worries, responsibilities, and obligations, it's difficult to be future minded. But we need to make a conscious effort. We need to let God stir up our faith. We need to start believing God for big things. We need to realize that even if the circumstances aren't so great today, God is bringing about a miracle in our future.

You see, no matter what you're dealing with today, God has a plan that will work things out better than you could ever imagine—if you'll just get your faith eyes in focus and become future minded. Ask God to help you change your focus.

The enemy doesn't want you to stand in faith for the fulfillment of your destiny. He doesn't want to see your children walking with God. He wants you to worry about all of the problems of today and forget about your future. Don't fall for the devil's plan. Focus on the future. See your children well and serving God. See your family happy and whole. Get a vision of victory today!

Lord, help me get my faith eyes in focus
and looking toward the future. Amen.

Say Yes to God

Teach me to do thy will; for thou art my God:
thy spirit is good; lead me into the land of uprightness.
PSALM 143:10 KJV

Have you come to a fork in your road of life? Do you feel God's call to serve? Do you recognize His voice and know it is Him? Simply wait on Him and say, "Yes."

Don't ponder over the what-ifs or whys, neither question your abilities. Don't worry about timing or the future. Test the calling to be sure it is of God. When you know it is Him, simply tell Him, "Yes."

When the mighty winds blow, He will miraculously place them at your back. When the floods begin to rage, He may tell you to keep paddling in faith, believing, while He calms the seas.

God's calling is sure. We don't have to worry about making a way. If it is His will, He works all things out in His own perfect way and timing.

He calls us through, around, over, and under to serve. No foe can stop us; no poverty can starve us; no evil can diminish His call. For He has a glorious plan!

So just say, "Yes."

From *When I'm Praising God*
ANITA CORRINE DONIHUE

Finding Balance

But the Lord said to her,
"My dear Martha, you are worried
and upset over all these details! There is only one thing
worth being concerned about. Mary has discovered it,
and it will not be taken away from her."
LUKE 10:41–42 NLT

With people in the house, needing to be fed, Martha jumped in to accomplish her tasks. Mary, on the other hand, chose to spend time in the presence of Jesus.

Because of Mary's choice, Martha had to do all the work by herself. She was even chastised for criticizing Mary. But if Martha hadn't done that work, who would have?

The two sisters from Bethany are a perfect example of the inner struggle that most women face daily. On one hand, we want to multitask and get things done. On the other hand, we crave rest, spiritual growth, and peace. The challenge is to blend the two into a healthy whole.

God has called us to good deeds, but not to stress and worry. Ask Him to show you the line.

Dear Lord, I want to do my part, like Martha—
but, like Mary, I also need to be strong enough
to say no, in order to have time with you.
Please show me how to find that balance in my life.

NICOLE O'DELL
From *Whispers of Wisdom for Single Moms*

The Big Picture

"As long as the earth endures, seedtime and harvest,
cold and heat, summer and winter,
day and night will never cease."
GENESIS 8:22

Somehow that verse is comforting to me. Just knowing that God can keep all of the earth's functions—seasons, temperatures, etc.—in order makes me feel good. Often I find myself stressing about time-related issues, such as: *Am I spending enough quality time with my children? Will I meet my book deadline? Will I have enough time to lose ten pounds before my next high school reunion?*

I recently heard a preacher on the radio talking about time management, and he asked, "Are you spinning your wheels or are you on a roll?"

Well, I thought, *it depends on which day you ask me!*

Some days I have it all together—everything is running on schedule and I feel in complete control. (Okay, realistically I have only three days a year like that.) Most of my days are filled with unexpected visitors, last-minute hair appointments, school activities, and putting out fires. Can I hear a collective "Amen"?

But we can rejoice in knowing that if God can keep the world spinning, He can certainly handle the tasks before us each day. So the next time you're running in circles, call on Him.

Lord, I recognize Your ability to keep everything in order.
I give every part of my life to You. Amen.